Lutheran Tradition as Heritage and Tool

CHURCH OF SWEDEN

Research Series

❧

Göran Gunner, editor
Vulnerability, Churches, and HIV (2009)

Kajsa Ahlstrand and Göran Gunner, editors
Non-Muslims in Muslim Majority Societies (2009)

Jonas Ideström, editor
For the Sake of the World (2010)

Göran Gunner and Kjell-Åke Nordquist
An Unlikely Dilemma (2011)

Anne-Louise Eriksson, Göran Gunner, and Niclas Blåder, editors
Exploring a Heritage (2012)

Kjell-Åke Nordquist, editor
Gods and Arms (2012)

Harald Hegstad
The Real Church (2013)

Carl-Henric Grenholm and Göran Gunners, editors
Justification in a Post-Christian Society (2014)

Carl-Henric Grenholm and Göran Gunner, editors
Lutheran Identity and Political Theology (2014)

Sune Fahlgren and Jonas Ideström, editors
Ecclesiology in the Trenches (2015)

Niclas Blåder
Lutheran Tradition as Heritage and Tool (2015)

Lutheran Tradition as Heritage and Tool

An Empirical Study of Reflections on Confessional Identity in Five Lutheran Churches in Different Contexts

NICLAS BLÅDER

☞PICKWICK *Publications* · Eugene, Oregon

LUTHERAN TRADITION AS HERITAGE AND TOOL
An Empirical Study of Reflections on Confessional Identity in Five Lutheran Churches in Different Contexts

Church of Sweden Research Series 11

Copyright © 2015 Trossamfundet Svenska kyrkan (Church of Sweden). All rights reserved. Except for brief quotations in critical publications or reviews, no part of this book may be reproduced in any manner without prior written permission form the publisher. Write: Permissions, Wipf and Stock Publishers, 199 W. 8th Ave., Suite 3, Eugene, OR 97401

Pickwick Publications
An Imprint of Wipf and Stock Publishers
199 W. 8th Ave., Suite 3
Eugene, OR 97401

www.wipfandstock.com

ISBN 13: 978-1-4982-2081-1

Cataloging-in-Publication data:

Blåder, Niclas

Lutheran tradition as heritage and tool : an empirical study of reflections on confessional identity in five Lutheran churches in different contexts / Niclas Blåder.

x + 180 p. ; 23 cm. —Includes bibliographical references.

Church of Sweden Research Series 11

ISBN 13: 978-1-4982-2081-1

1. Lutheran Church—Costa Rica. 2. Lutheran Church—Brazil. 3. Lutheran Church—Iceland. 4. Lutheran Church—Indonesia. 5. Lutheran Church—Madagascar. I. Series. II. Title.

BX8065.2 B4 2015

Manufactured in the U.S.A.

Scripture quotations are from New Revised Standard Version Bible, copyright © 1989 National Council of the Churches of Christ in the United States of America. Used by permission. All rights reserved.

Contents

Preface   ix

1. Introduction   1

An Example That Ends with a Broader Question   1
In Transition   5
A Lutheran Folk Church   6
Shaped through Handling Dilemmas   8
A Confessional Understanding and *Semper Reformanda*   9
Lutheranism and Global Christianity   11
The Beginning of a Question   12

2. The Way Forward   14

Dilemmas   14
Making the Question More Specific   16
Countries and Churches   17
Questions   18
Interviews and Papers   20
Images of the Churches   22
Self-Reflections   23
Structure and Purpose   25
Some Ethical Considerations   26

3. Five Churches   27

Costa Rica—Iglesia Lutherana Costaricense, ILCO   27
   Being a Sign of Hope   28
   A Church without Walls   32
   The Religious Context   35
   Women's Situation   37
   Leadership   39
   Theological Foundations   41
   Summary   43

Brazil—Igreja Evangélica de Confissão Lutherana no Brasil, IECLB 44
    Identity Foundations 46
    Brazil's Religious Setting 47
    The Way to Be Church 52
    Women's Situation 56
    Theology 58
    Summary 60
Iceland—Þjóðkirkjan, (ELCI) 61
    A National or a Folk Church 63
    The Church and Iceland Today 65
    Being a Lutheran Church 67
    Structure and Leadership 69
    Women's Situation 71
    Summary 72
Madagascar—Fiangonana Loterana Malagasy, FLM 73
    The Identity Base 74
    Fifohazana 80
    Women's Situation 85
    Structure and Leadership 87
    Summary 88
Indonesia—Huria Kristen Batak Protestan, HKBP 89
    Foundation of the Church 91
    The Influence of Charismatic Movements 96
    Church and Culture 99
    A Muslim Majority Society 100
    Women's Situation 101
    Summary 103

4. Living with Contradictions 105

Four Dilemmas
Community *and* Pluralism 106
    The IECLB, Brazil—Transformation from an Ethnic Church 106
    The FLM, Madagascar—Finding New Ways to Include Pluralism 107
    How Bonhoeffer Addresses the Dilemma 108
    The Situation in the IECLB Seen in Relation to Bonhoeffer 114
    The Situation in the FLM Seen in Relation to Bonhoeffer 116
Power *and* Servanthood 119
    The ELCI, Iceland—Bringing a Powerful History 119
    The ILCO, Costa Rica—Empowering the Powerless 120
    How Sykes Addresses the Dilemma 120
    The Situation in the ELCI Seen in Relation to Sykes 126
    The Situation in the ILCO Seen in Relation to Sykes 129

Alternative to Culture *and* Affirmative of Culture 130
    The HKBP, Indonesia—A Chosen and a Forced Culture 131
    The IECLB, Brazil—An Including Way 132
    How Niebuhr Addresses the Dilemma 132
    The Situation in the HKBP Seen in Relation to Niebuhr 136
    The Situation in the IECLB Seen in Relation to Niebuhr 139
Inward *and* Outward 140
    The HKBP, Indonesia—Boundaries 141
    The ILCO, Costa Rica—Community as a Way to Reach Out 142
    How Moltmann Addresses the Dilemma 142
    The Situation in the HKBP Seen in Relation to Moltmann 147
    The Situation in the ILCO Seen in Relation to Moltmann 148
A Few Reflections 151
    Responsible, Relevant, and Authentic 151

5. *Tradition as a Tool* 153

Doctrine of the Two Kingdoms 154
Doctrine of the Universal Priesthood 156
The Vocation 158
Doctrine of Justification 159
A Problematic Discrepancy 161
    A Need for a Critical Dialogue with Tradition 162
    A Need for a Critical Dialogue with Other Lutheran Churches 165
Challenges For the Future 166
    The Importance of Taking the Situation Seriously 166
    The Importance of Using Tradition as a Critical partner 167
    The Importance of a Constant, Ongoing Conversation 167
    Meeting the Challenges 168

Appendix, Questionnaire 171

Sources and Bibliography 175

Preface

This book is the result of a long process and help from many people. The project started when I was newly employed and Associate Professor Anne-Louise Eriksson was heading the research unit. I would like to thank her, my colleague Associate Professor Göran Gunner, and my former colleague Hanna Stenström, who all, in various degrees, have been working together with me, making interviews and arranging for research papers to be written in the different countries. They have also read the text at various stages, contributing with critical eyes.

I would also like to thank Associate Professor Edgar Almén, PhD Jan Eckerdal, and my colleagues at Church of Sweden Research Unit, as well as at Church of Sweden Unit for Analysis, for many discussions and constructive criticism. The Department for Theology and Public Witness (DTPW) at the Lutheran World Federation (LWF) in Geneva has given important comments, as have many people at academic presentations and presentations in Church of Sweden. Many thanks goes also to the unknown peer reviewer who, towards the end of the process, has made substantial contributions to improving the text on every level.

Language editor Patrick Hort has in a very professional way made my poor English into something more readable. And my fiancée Anna Menzies has continuously read the text and helped to make it understandable for more people than myself.

Most of all I would like to thank the representatives of the five churches that generously participated in this study. Without their willingness to discuss their churches and the obstacles and possibilities they see, this book would never have seen the light of day.

Niclas Blåder
Nyköping 2015

1

Introduction

AN EXAMPLE THAT ENDS WITH A BROADER QUESTION

Some time ago, a friend of mine was looking for a picture of Martin Luther in the Church of Sweden's central photo archive and could not find one. This may seem both peculiar and strange—but not important. But it could also raise a larger question about what it means to be a Lutheran church and how this affects decisions and actions in the church.

This book has its origins in my home arena, the Church of Sweden. It is by looking at what is well known and familiar that broader questions arise. So, while the starting point is the Church of Sweden, that does not mean that it is only about the Church of Sweden. The essence of what is to be found in these first pages is probably evident in many Lutheran churches around the world.[1]

In this chapter the study's background will be spelled out with a brief presentation of the Church of Sweden in relation to its Lutheran heritage. This presentation opens up for a wider global perspective and the chapter ends with the study's fundamental question.

The Church of Sweden understands itself as a Lutheran church and relates to other churches as a Lutheran church. But what does the Lutheran heritage mean for contemporary Church of Sweden? This question has no simple answer and different opinions are articulated in the church.

---

1. Other studies in English that can broaden the picture of the Church of Sweden or provide information from another angle are, for example, Ryman et al., *Nordic Folk Churches*; Eriksson et al., *Exploring a Heritage*.

Examples can be found by following what is said at church seminars, reading articles or listening to sermons. Another way is to peruse the motions for the annual General Synod of the Church of Sweden; they almost invariably include motions that highlight Luther and the Lutheran heritage more explicitly. One of the motions in 2011, "Luther i fem år" [Luther for Five Years] by Leif Nordlander,[2] proposed that each year's delegates to the General Synod should hear a lecture about the Church of Sweden's Lutheran Identity; that the Central Board should publish a series on Lutheran theology and also develop material for the Luther Jubilee in 2017; finally, the Central Board should in 2017 arrange a celebration to commemorate the Reformation. The motion also included a brief motivation of the proposals:

> 2017 is a milestone in the Lutheran world. It is 500 years since Martin Luther nailed the theses to the church door in Wittenberg. The German Lutheran church is at the forefront with their plans. Their Luther Decade—ten years of considering Luther from theological, historical and other aspects—started in 2007. We ought to be able to do the same for five years and deepen our identity as an Evangelical Lutheran church. The Church of Sweden has a weak Lutheran identity. In society in general, people often blame "Luther" for poor self-esteem and depression without eliciting any protests from the Church of Sweden. Prejudices about Lutheran theology also go unchallenged. This results in a distorted and slightly negative picture of the theology that makes up the Church of Sweden's foundation. It also creates uncertainty in ecumenical contacts, when the lack of theological self-awareness leads to fear in the encounter with people of other Christian traditions. I can, after participating in schools in Bavaria, note that children in German elementary schools probably know at least as much or more about Luther and his life than the average priest in the Church of Sweden. The newly resigned Bishop of Gothenburg, Carl Axel Aurelius, along with Pastor Margareta Brandby-Cöster, presented a new interpretation of the *Small Catechism* which has now been published with an easily accessible "Introduction" by Aurelius and a study guide by Brandby-Cöster. Let us have more such books.[3]

The motion is critical of what its author considers to be characteristic of the situation in the Church of Sweden. There is little, if any, knowledge of Luther and Lutheran theology. The observation that German elementary schoolchildren have better knowledge of Luther than the average Swedish

---

2. Nordlander, "Luther i fem år."
3. Ibid. My translation.

priest is something that the Church of Sweden must take seriously and try to change.

A year earlier, in 2010, another motion, "Bekännelseskrifterna och ekumeniska överenskommelser" [Confessional Documents and Ecumenical Agreements] by Jan-Anders Ekelund and Håkan Sunnliden,[4] proposed that every delegate to the General Synod should get a personal copy of the Church of Sweden's confessional writings and ecumenical agreements, on the grounds that it could prove dangerous for a church to have a highest decision-making body with delegates who lack a proper knowledge of its confessional writings. The motion's authors considered that decisions in an Evangelical Lutheran church need to be well-informed by Evangelical Lutheran theology and the church's confessional writings.

The opinion that there is a lack of knowledge about Luther and Lutheranism in church—as well as in society—and that discussions and decisions in the Church of Sweden suffer from this is not confined to the authors of these motions. In the preface to *Människohjärtat och bibeln* [The Human Heart and the Bible], Professor Birgit Stolt writes that her reason for writing the book is to give a picture of Luther that differs from what is normally seen in Sweden today, which is often badly informed and conveys a negative image.[5] In the book she exemplifies how the image of Luther changed in Sweden between 1930 and 1980[6] and goes on to try and understand why this happened and to construct a different picture. This description of the situation for Lutheranism in Sweden and the Church of Sweden has, however, been questioned by Professor Mattias Martinson at Uppsala University, who points out that even if knowledge of Luther is low in an active sense, Lutheranism has impregnated Swedish society in such a way that it is impossible to live in Sweden without coming into contact with the Lutheranism that is embedded in Swedish society. One could say that not even a secular, not to say atheistic, Swede can avoid the grip of Lutheranism.[7]

In the middle of the last century the situation was different. Professor Gustaf Wingren's dissertation *Luthers lära om kallelsen*,[8] [Luther on Vocation] from 1942, was just one of a series of dissertations or articles that dealt

4. Ekelund and Sunnliden, "Bekännelseskrifterna."
5. Stolt, *Martin Luther*, 7–8.
6. Ibid., 13–19.
7. Martinson, *Katedralen mitt i staden*.
8. Wingren, *Luthers lära om kallelsen*.

with either Luther or Lutheran theology at Sweden's theological faculties. In the preface to the fourth edition, from 1992, Wingren wrote that he had been a student to the great Luther scholars Nathan Söderblom and Einar Billing, who had made Luther an honorable name in Swedish church life.[9] Some years after Wingren's dissertation, and for various reasons, other subjects in the theological curriculum—not least the theology of Karl Barth, Dietrich Bonhoeffer, and Paul Tillich—started to attract interest and Luther ceased to be the figure whom anyone aspiring to an academic career ought to write about. While Luther did not, of course, lose his leading position among theologians, he was not studied in the same way as before. This is now changing by degrees and there seems to be a new interest in Luther and Lutheran theology. An example is the research project *Lutheran Theology and Ethics in a Post-Christian Society*, led from the Department of Theology at Uppsala University, which in time will result in a number of publications that focus on Lutheran theology. A renewed interest is also evident in the Church of Sweden, with conferences and discussions.[10]

People's relations with Luther and the Lutheran tradition have taken and still take many forms in Sweden. The question of Luther's impact on Swedish society has also been discussed, for instance in *Luther i Sverige* [Luther in Sweden], by Carl Axel Aurelius, professor and former Bishop of Gothenburg. His starting point is a lecture by the Danish Church historian Poul Georg Lindhardt, claiming that Luther's importance for the Nordic reformation was not so great. For Aurelius this was a challenging claim and he discusses the Swedish situation with reference to the Reformation Jubilees in the seventeenth, eighteenth, and nineteenth centuries. In contrast to Lindhardt, he concludes that Luther has had a tremendous impact on Swedish society and points to three findings. Luther's writings were important firstly in the formation of the confessional state, secondly in the destruction of the confessional state and thirdly when modern Swedish society was coming into being. Aurelius considers that Luther's writings could be understood as "classics" in Swedish society. They have been there for a very long time and during that time they have been involved in both the construction and the deconstruction of church and society.[11] Aurelius'

---

9. Ibid., 7.

10. Examples are the various arrangements for the Reformation Jubilee, to be held in 2017. Another example is the international conference, "Remembering the Past—Living the Future. Lutheran Tradition in Transition," arranged by the Church of Sweden Research Unit together with the Department of Theology at Uppsala University in 2013.

11. Aurelius, *Luther i Sverige*, 167.

book ends with the Reformation Jubilee in 1817. That was almost 200 years ago and the Church of Sweden now looks different.

IN TRANSITION

Today, the Church of Sweden is the world's largest Lutheran church, with more than six million members. There are almost 1400 parishes and 3100 ordained priests[12] in the thirteen dioceses. Almost 70 percent of the population belongs to the church.[13] The name "Church of Sweden" tells a story about a church that has had a tremendous impact on people and society for a very long time. Before the mid-nineteenth century no other churches were permitted in Sweden[14] and religious freedom was not granted until 1951.

The Church of Sweden has a democratic structure.[15] From the sixteenth century until the year 2000 it was connected to the state by law. The priests were employed by the church but were at the same time civil servants. Up until the mid-1990s, the Church of Sweden was also responsible for the civil registration of all citizens. Moreover, bishops were appointed by the government, acting on proposals from the church. Today the situation is different. The Church of Sweden is still subject to a law that regulates its relationship with the state but essentially it is a church that decides its internal affairs. The main decision-making body is the General Synod, with 251 delegates who meet annually. They are chosen in general elections every fourth year by the members of the Church of Sweden, but the actual numbers who vote are low.[16] There is a similar democratic structure in every diocese and parish.

12. "Arbeta som präst."
13. "Svenska kyrkan i siffror."
14. See for example Gustafsson, *Svensk kyrkohistoria*, 207–38.
15. In The Church of Sweden Act (SFS 1998:1591) which contains fourteen paragraphs, the second one reads, "Church of Sweden is an open folk church, that in cooperation between a democratic organization and the ministry of the church conducts a nationwide operation." How the word democratic is to be understood was not discussed at length before the separation of church and state in 2000, but afterwards the role of democracy has been discussed several times in the Church of Sweden, not least in a study introduced in 2003 by the Church of Sweden Church Board. Eriksson et al., *Demokratin är en successiv uppenbarelse*.
16. The proportion who voted in the 2013 election was 12 percent. See "Tillsammans gör vi kyrkovalet."

Some of the challenges being discussed today concern the low knowledge of Christian belief and the Bible in society in general. Another challenge is that membership is declining at an annual rate of approximately 50,000 persons. The numbers of baptisms, marriages, and funerals in the church are falling slowly but steadily. Also the voice of the church in political or public debate is not as strong as it once was and the role of the church in the cultural sphere is in many ways weakening, too. Discussions about organization and structure that could meet these challenges are plentiful and considered important.

Swedish society has also changed from an agricultural set-up 150 years ago to an industrialized society and today's economically diversified society. This development has been accompanied by democratization. Universal suffrage was granted and trade unions started to develop along with other social movements. At the same time, other churches appeared and spread. The Church of Sweden is still by far the largest, but a variety of Christian voices are heard today and quite a few of them are immigrants. Sweden society has become much more multicultural. Almost one and a half million out of Sweden's nine and a half million were born abroad. This is enriching Sweden but it also gives rise to political disputes and discussions. The long-term changes in the political, social, and religious landscapes have been accompanied by trends towards secularization and individualization. In the international Inglehart-Welzel surveys, Sweden excels—together with the other Nordic countries—as a country in which Secular-Rational values and Self Expression values are ranked very high.[17] Secularization and individualization are not unambiguous concepts, either in everyday speech or when used scientifically, so it is difficult to pin down their importance in Sweden and the Church of Sweden. A common interpretation includes the displacement of religion in society. Another interpretation focuses on how the "great stories," along with shared images and religious authorities, lose their meaning in favor of individual perspectives. Regardless of how the concepts are interpreted, it is clear that Swedish society is constantly changing.

A LUTHERAN FOLK CHURCH

In the Church Ordinance, which constitutes the Church of Sweden's statutes, two concepts seem to be central: "Evangelical Lutheran"[18] and "folk

17. Inglehart and Welzel, "WVS Cultural Map of the World."
18. *Kyrkoordningen*, Part I, chapter 1.

church."[19] The Church of Sweden has for a century understood itself as a "folk Church"[20] and continues to do so. The concept is elusive but can be said to indicate that the church sees itself as not just, or predominantly, a church for those who are actively seeking access to church activities and worship. How and in what ways people respond to the call of God is hidden to all but God. The central concept is therefore God's grace, not the active human response.[21] In *Folkkyrkans kropp* [The Body of the Folk Church], Jan Eckerdal describes the Swedish folk church largely as a church where the community aspect is, to some extent, neglected for church life.[22] Eckerdal puts this in simple terms by saying that the Word of grace goes from God to the priest or other church employees and from them to the parishioners. What matters is the individual being reached by God's grace. According to Eckerdal, in the folk church model, the church community is not a necessary tool for accomplishing this.[23] One consequence of this is that the Church of Sweden is a church where the congregations encompass the whole country, thereby fulfilling its mission of making God's grace reach everyone. The Church of Sweden is the Church of *Sweden*, not least because its field of work is the whole of Sweden. Every citizen has access to the churches and their activities.[24] In a central section, the Church Ordinance underlines this by citing openness and inclusiveness as central in the Church of Sweden's self-understanding.

> The Church of Sweden is an open folk church with the mission to communicate the Gospel in word and deed. The church has room for everyone, for seekers and for those who doubt, as well as for those who are strong in faith, for those who have not come as far, as well as for those who have advanced further on the path of faith.[25] Besides being an open folk church, the Church Ordinance states that the Church of Sweden is an Evangelical Lutheran church.

> The Church of Sweden's faith, confession and doctrine, shaped through liturgy and life, are grounded in God's holy word as given

19. Ibid., Part VI, Introduction.
20. For further reading about the concept "folk-church" in a Nordic setting, see for example: Eriksson et al., *Exploring a Heritage*.
21. Billing, *Den svenska folkkyrkan*.
22. Eckerdal, *Folkkyrkans kropp*, 91–97, 278–90.
23. Ibid., 335–38.
24. *Kyrkoordningen*, Part II, Introduction.
25. Ibid., Part VI, Introduction. My translation.

in the prophetic and apostolic writings of the Old and New Testament and summarized in the Apostolic, Nicene, and Athanasian creeds and in the unchanged Augsburg Confession from 1530, confirmed and acknowledged in the decisions of the Uppsala Synod in 1593, explained and commented upon in the Book of Concord and other documents acknowledged by the Church of Sweden.[26]

The Lutheran history of the Church of Sweden started in 1516 when the Swede Olaus Petri came to Leipzig in Germany. He soon moved to the relatively new university in Wittenberg, to which Martin Luther had come in 1512, and was still there when Luther nailed his ninety-five theses to the door of the castle church. Later, Olaus Petri became an important person in Swedish church life; partly due to his own efforts but mainly to historical circumstances. The most important factor was the election of a new king, Gustav Wasa, in 1523, initially with the support of the church hierarchy. However, the ideas about a strong monarchy that reached Sweden from Wittenberg fitted the new king's plans and the church's relations with the king became tenser. Olaus Petri became secretary to the City of Stockholm, an office that involved preaching in the cathedral.[27] The reformation in Sweden took place in the decades that followed. A Swedish translation of the New Testament appeared in 1526 and a translation of the whole Bible in 1541. A number of other writings, influenced by Luther, were also published at this time. Laurentius Petri, Olaus Petri's brother, became Archbishop of Sweden in 1531, the first without papal sanction. The reformation in Sweden was not a single, definitive event so much as a movement that took different guises, depending on political and religious circumstances. It was not until the Uppsala Synod in 1593 that the church was labeled Evangelical Lutheran. The reformation in Sweden was then completed—by royal decree—in 1611.[28] The Church of Sweden has understood itself ever since as a Lutheran church.

SHAPED THROUGH HANDLING DILEMMAS

As indicated above, the Church of Sweden has taken its historical legacy into each new situation, a legacy that has been constantly reshaped over the years in order to be passed on to the next generation. Over and over again,

---

26. Ibid., Part I, 1 §. My translation.
27. Ingebrand, "Olavus Petri—reformatorn," 13–16.
28. Gustafsson, *Svensk kyrkohistoria*, 81–91.

the talk about what the church is or should be has been negotiated and renegotiated in the encounter between its heritage and the ways in which it has chosen to respond to upcoming challenges. The answers have never been homogeneous or constant. Rather, they have represented many faces, constantly evolving and changing.

It would not be wrong to say that today's Church of Sweden has to some extent been shaped by its solutions to the problems it has faced. Problems that have sometimes turned out to be more than that (i.e., dilemmas). By this I mean problems that could not be dealt with in practice without the solution doing away with other things that are also considered correct and good. Whatever the decision, there will be losses as well as gains. In facing such dilemmas, the Church of Sweden has created a very specific, Swedish idea of what being Lutheran means. This is evident, not least, in questions concerning democracy in the church, creating a Swedish view of how a church ought to be organized, structured and led.[29] It is also evident in the aforementioned example of Einar Billing and the creation of a folk church. This has brought specific perceptions of Lutheranism into the church, not least thoughts about radical openness.[30] Another example is the formation of the unitary state of Sweden, in which Lutheranism has been used to separate the material from the spiritual. Sweden's Luther—like the Luther of all churches—is a specific Luther, formed by specific problems and dilemmas over a long period. This has made the Luther of today, as seen in Sweden, not just Swedish but in many respects also a twentieth century construction.[31] Even today, at every level in the Church of Sweden—in parishes, dioceses and at the national level—dilemmas are constantly being handled, making it evolve.

A CONFESSIONAL UNDERSTANDING AND *SEMPER REFORMANDA*

However, from the Church of Sweden's long history of being a Lutheran church it does not follow that everyone understands what that means. Nor does it follow that there is, or should be, a single understanding of how that heritage should be interpreted.

---

29. For a discussion about questions of democracy in the Church of Sweden see for example, Eriksson et al., *Demokratin är en succesiv uppenbarelse*.

30. See for example Eckerdal, *Folkkyrkans kropp*.

31. See for example Claesson, "Att lösa klimatproblem."

In the article "The Construction of Lutheran identity in the Church of Sweden," Thomas Ekstrand—inspired by Ragnar Holte—distinguishes between two ideal types of Lutheran identity that he uses to categorize an empirical material: a *confessional* type and a *semper reformanda* type.[32] He makes clear that they are both to be understood as ideal types and that neither of them is therefore normally to be found in a pure form. In the confessional sense, Luther's theology is important in itself. The church constantly needs to return to, and have some agreement with, the central theological concepts Luther worked with.[33] The *semper reformanda* sense could be said to focus on an ongoing reformation such as Luther performed when protesting against the authorities and powers.[34] Ekstrand discerns the two ways of relating to Luther when he analyses different forms for expressing the identity of the Church of Sweden. He concludes that it is possible to find things that are correct in both types, but he also sees problems with both of them. In the Confessional sense it is sometimes the case that a part of Luther's theology is highlighted in a one-sided way; as an example he mentions the doctrine of justification. Luther's theology is reduced to one or a few dogmatic standpoints and nothing more.[35] But he also notes that there are problems with the *semper reformanda* sense as well.

> The *semper reformanda* type often uses Luther in order to argue for a church that is ready to reform itself in order to be relevant in contemporary culture. This is also an exaggeration of some traits in Luther's theological outlook. It is of course true that Luther was sharply opposed to the ecclesiastical authorities and traditions of his time. But he did not perceive this criticism as the center of his theology. Rather it was a consequence of his deeply conservative theological method—he thought that the church of his time had abandoned the original and true Christian faith, to which it ought to return again and again.[36]

These two different ways of relating to, and understanding, the Lutheran heritage in the Church of Sweden has both strengths and weaknesses. But neither of them alone gives a complete picture of the Lutheran

---

32. Ekstrand, "Construction of Lutheran Identity," 249–64; Holte, *Luther och Lutherbilden*, 19–21.

33. Ekstrand, "Construction of Lutheran Identity," 256.

34. Ibid.

35. Ibid., 260–61.

36. Ibid., 261.

heritage and how it should affect the church. There is a tension between them and each one needs to inform the other to some extent, according to Ekstrand.[37]

LUTHERANISM AND GLOBAL CHRISTIANITY

Throughout the history of Christianity, churches have discussed who they are, what they believe, how they should act and what people ought to believe in order to be a member. In the article, "Om att lära sig vara i minoritet—men ändå vara glad" [About how to learn how to be in minority—but nevertheless be happy], Jan Eckerdal tries to explain the situation by saying that ever since the cross, the Christian question has been: What are we going to do now?[38] The cross put the disciples in the unfamiliar and disturbing situation of having a leader who had died. The situation differed from what they thought or hoped for: What are we going to do now? On the third day he was alive again: What are we going to do now? Soon after, he said he would leave them but that God will send them another Comforter, and the disciples once again had to ask: What are we going to do now? That question has followed the Christian church down the centuries and has been answered differently by different churches in different times. But it has always been answered.

Two thousand years and many, many different answers later, Christianity has grown into the world's largest religion with about two billion members divided into 35,000 separate churchly organizations covering the whole world. Almost all of them are affiliated to one of the four major traditions that we can see in the world today: Eastern Orthodox (11.5 percent), Roman Catholic (50 percent), Protestant (21 percent), and the Pentecostal/Charismatic movement (17.5 percent).[39] These four main traditions can then be divided into subgroups. The Protestants number almost 400 million and the greater part of them belong to either the Anglican, the Baptist, the Lutheran, the Methodist or the Reformed tradition.

As its name indicates, the Protestant tradition is at least to some extent a protest movement with its roots in sixteenth century reformers' criticism of how the Roman Catholic Church acted and what it believed. But Protestant can also denote "to confess" what one believes in. However, Protestant is not the only label for this group; in some parts of the world

37. Ibid., 261–62.
38. Eckerdal, "Om att lära sig vara i minoritet."
39. Jacobsen, *World's Christians*, 8.

Protestants are named Evangelicals instead, which can lead to misunderstandings. The word evangelical is used differently in different parts of the world and in different churches.[40] For example, the Church of Sweden is an Evangelical Lutheran church but what that stands for is very different from what is meant in some other countries by saying that one is evangelical. A major section of the Protestant tradition is the Lutheran sub-tradition. Today, approximately 70 million people belong to the Lutheran tradition and they are spread all over the world. Most of them are also members of churches that belong to the Lutheran World Federation (LWF), which has 142 member churches. But the shared Lutheran heritage does not mean that all of them understand what that means in the same way. Churches in the LWF, though standing on a common ground, reflect and act differently, sometimes even contradictorily.[41]

Churches have always been challenged by the theology and praxis of other churches. The ecumenical movement has therefore aimed to understand and overcome differences in order to help churches towards visible unity and to fulfill the church's mission in the world. The challenge is present not only between churches that belong to different traditions but also between those that belong to the same "church family" or confession.[42] Due to historical circumstances and contexts, churches have developed diverse ways of acting and of understanding and interpreting Scripture and tradition. This has sometimes been a help and sometimes a source of misunderstandings and questions. It is a help when a church sees other churches develop a practice and/or teaching that contributes to a better understanding of its own calling and mission, and a source of questions when it sees other churches developing a practice and/or a teaching that it perceives as strange or incomprehensible.

THE BEGINNING OF A QUESTION

As has been shown above, the Church of Sweden's Lutheran heritage and Lutheran self-understanding have been important historically and are important today. At the same time, its self-understanding is in many ways vague. The Lutheran heritage is central for how the Church of Sweden

---

40. Ibid., 39.
41. Grietsch, *History of Lutheranism*.
42. A major work that relates to this study was done by LWF between 1997 and 2000, discussing what ecclesiology means, how it is lived in different churches and what LWF as a communion means in relation to that. Greive, *Between Vision and Reality*.

describes itself and for how it is officially understood; this is frequently evident not least in official documents and when the larger story of the church is told. But what it means to be a Lutheran church is not always as easy to describe as to say that one is one. Church of Sweden has been a Lutheran Church for around 500 years but how is that to be interpreted and how does the Lutheran heritage affect what is happening today in the church? There seems to be a discrepancy between the importance of the Lutheran heritage in the Church of Sweden and the vague understanding of what that heritage means today.

One way to reflect on this could be to open up for a larger or broader discussion by looking at some other Lutheran churches. If questions about the Lutheran heritage and what it means to be Lutheran are to be found in the Church of Sweden, similar discussions are probably to be found also in other Lutheran churches. And today, when Lutheranism is a global phenomenon, an adequate question to ask for any Lutheran church could be: what does the Lutheran heritage mean in other churches and in what way does it affect their decisions and activities? Is the same phenomenon, with an important but vague Lutheran self understanding, to be seen also there? How do they relate to their heritage? And in what way does it affect their actions? The answers to these questions ought to be interesting for a wider circle of Lutheran churches, with a potential to inform also their reflections about their own churches.

2

The Way Forward

An overall aim of this study is to discuss what it means to be a Lutheran church in today's world. To be able to do this, a partial aim of this study is to describe five Lutheran churches in different parts of the world. Instead of doing this by applying a sociological method, the description is made up of theoretical reflections by persons who have leading positions in their churches. These self-reflections are complemented by interviews and papers written by researchers. Another partial aim, building on the first one, is to analyze and discuss the material to see whether, and if so, in what way Lutheran theology is used in decisions and actions when the churches are dealing with their situations.

DILEMMAS

When the study was planned, the intention was to start with the confessional identity, which was thought to be clarified in the interviews, but it turned out that such an identity was hard to detect in the material. Instead of describing their Lutheran heritage and what that heritage meant for them today, the informants answered the questions mainly by talking about their church's burning issues. The material therefore had to be approached in a different way.

When analyzing the material it became evident that all five churches were involved in handling a few dilemmas. By dilemmas I mean problems that do not have a single, definitive solution. They are something that each church has to deal with over and over again in an unending procedure, never being able to arrive at a solution which everyone understands as good and relevant.

These dilemmas are not confined to just one or some of the churches, while others are dealing with different dilemmas. The material shows that, in one way or another, all the five churches are struggling with the same types of dilemma but are doing so in different situations. They have different histories and different traditions, so their solutions also differ. But it is not just these churches that face these dilemmas; they are rather to be understood as general Christian dilemmas. In other words, they are to be found not only in Lutheran churches or today, but also in other denominations and throughout Christian history.

The dilemmas I choose to highlight are not the only ones in the material, but they are found in all five churches and are distinct and clear. These dilemmas could be described as how to handle—in the best way for each church—the relationship between (1) "community *and* pluralism," (2) "power *and* servanthood," (3) "how to be an alternative to culture *and* being affirmative to culture," and (4) "how to handle being both inward *and* outward." A Christian church should be creating communities at the same time as it is open to diversity and pluralism. It should both be a servant and have power, it should live in the culture at the same time as it should be an alternative to it, it should be reaching in to the core community at the same time as it is reaching out, acting responsibly. Other dilemmas, such as that of "tradition *and* renewal," could also have been chosen, but the first four will suffice for the purpose of showing how the churches handle dilemmas.

These dilemmas are often aired in systematic theological discussions and will therefore be spelled out and discussed with the help of four well-known theologians. The four dilemmas are to be understood as general in the Christian tradition and have consequently been discussed by many. Thus, the choice of these four theologians is not to be understood as implying that they are the only ones or those that have dealt with this topic most explicitly. They are rather to be understood as representatives of a huge, systematic theological discussion. Each of the chosen theologians is well-known, they are important for many and also for the theological debate in general. And each one of them has in some way addressed at least one of these dilemmas in a book. For the relation between community *and* pluralism, *Life Together* by Dietrich Bonhoeffer will be used. The relation between power *and* servanthood will be presented through Stephen Sykes and his book *Power and Christian Theology*. The relation between being an alternative to culture *and* being affirmative to culture is viewed through H. Richard Niebuhr's book *Christ & Culture*. Lastly, the relation between inwardly *and* outwardly is presented by Jürgen Moltmann and *The Church in the Power of the Spirit*. That the chosen theologians belong to different churches and theological traditions is not of importance for this study. This means that a choice of other theologians would not affect the result in principle, as long as the chosen theologians see the dilemmas as dilemmas instead of as easily solved problems. The four theologians function as examples of theological discussions about how to handle a dilemma in practical church life, not as guides to how it should be done in a good, indisputable or Lutheran way.

The chosen theologians are all male and centered in Europe or the United States. Other choices could of course have been made. The aim has been to find theologians who have influenced the theological debate in general and who at the same time are theologians that all the churches probably take seriously and want to be in dialogue with. Moreover, they have all addressed the dilemmas in ways that relate to real church life, that is, they are in some way trying to combine theology and praxis in what they are doing.

By throwing light on the different dilemmas each church is handling and then see this in relation to a theological discussion, I am able to discern what turns out to be of importance for the churches in their reflections about how to handle the dilemmas.

MAKING THE QUESTION MORE SPECIFIC

The large question is what the Lutheran heritage means and how it affects decisions and activities in a few Lutheran churches, which is examined by looking at how the churches are handling dilemmas that confront them. This question is made more specific by relating the discussion about the dilemmas to what was said in the previous chapter by theologian Thomas Ekstrand about the relation between a confessional understanding and a *semper reformanda* understanding.

> The *semper reformanda* type would argue that being an Evangelical Lutheran church today means being prepared to live in constant reformation according to the Protestant principle exemplified by the reformers' courage in challenging the authorities of their time, which made it possible to proclaim the gospel in freedom. The confessional type would argue that being an Evangelical Lutheran

church today must mean being in some sort of agreement with the central theological convictions of sixteenth century Lutheran theology and church practice.[1]

According to Ekstrand, both ways of relating to the Lutheran heritage ought to be present and they need to inform each other. But he also sees that one of the two is often understood as more important than the other. The confessional and the *semper reformanda* understandings are sometimes seen as two rather separate ways of relating to the Lutheran heritage, even if, according to Ekstrand, they never or seldom are found in a pure form.[2]

What information does the empirical material in this study provide about this? Is it possible to see whether the churches are leaning towards a confessional understanding or a *semper reformanda* understanding of the Lutheran heritage? Do both understandings affect each other or inform each other in a constructive way? Or do the churches preferably lean towards one of the two?

COUNTRIES AND CHURCHES

The Lutheran world is vast and diversified. Some member churches in the LWF have almost seven million members, others just a few thousand. Some were founded by missionaries in the nineteenth century, others began without missionary efforts. Some exist in economically prosperous areas, others in developing countries. There are old churches and very young churches.

Among all these different types, five churches have been selected for this study: Iglesia Lutherana Costarricense (the ILCO) in Costa Rica, Igreja Evangélica de Confissão Lutherana no Brasil (the IECLB) in Brazil, the Evangelical Lutheran Church in Iceland (The ELCI) in Iceland, Fiangonana Loterana Malagasy (the FLM) in Madagascar, and Huria Kristen Batak Protestan (the HKBP) in Indonesia.[3] The choice has been discussed and made in cooperation with the International Department and the Ecumenical Unit at the Church of Sweden and the Department for Theology

---

1. Ekstrand, "Construction of Lutheran Identity," 256.
2. Ibid., 249–64.
3. In the text, in all but one case I will use the abbreviations of the churches' names in their own languages, abbreviations which the churches themselves use: Iglesia Lutherana Costarricense—ILCO, Igreja Evangélica de Confissão Lutherana no Brasil—IECLB, Fiangonana Loterana Malagasy—FLM, and Huria Kristen Batak Protestant—HKBP. The exception, for which I will use the English abbreviation, is the Evangelical Lutheran Church in Iceland—ELCI—because there is no abbreviation in Icelandic.

and Public Witness (DTPW) at the Lutheran World Federation (LWF). The main consideration has been to include churches of different types. The five churches manifest this diversity: they are from different parts of the world; some are small, others larger; some are old, others of more recent origin; some were founded by missionaries, others were not. These churches also differ in their organization and how to be and to act. In short, the chosen churches are good examples of what the Lutheran world looks like today. It should be added that to some extent the choice has been guided by practical circumstances. All five churches are churches with which the Church of Sweden has been in contact for a long time or been relatively easy to contact. Finally, the choices have, of course, been made among churches which, at the time, had the ability and the interest to take part in this study.

A choice of other countries and other churches might have led to different results. However, the purpose of this study has not been to arrive at all the various ways of handling Lutheranism in the LWF or to discuss a specific way of handling the Lutheran heritage. The countries and the churches in this study present a variety that must be understood as relevant for the present purpose.

QUESTIONS

From the very beginning there have been four questions around which the study has circled. However, the main focus is on how Lutheran identity is constructed today. The other three questions are used to inform this one. These four questions have functioned as core questions, structuring the interviews.

- How is Lutheran identity constructed today?
- How are churches affected by the globally growing Pentecostal or Charismatic influences?
- What is the situation for women? And what theology underpins their situation within the churches?
- What can be said to be present-day "burning issues," and how are they a part of the formation and identity of the church?

There have been various reasons for choosing these four main questions but in general it can be said that they all yield important information about how the different churches understand themselves. That is, with the help of the secondary questions under each of the four main questions and by putting relevant but not pre-decided questions during the semi-structured interviews, it is possible to get at something of each church's self-understanding and thereby form a picture of each church.[4]

The background to the first and main question—How is Lutheran identity constructed today?—is that identity has become an important concept for understanding what is happening in the world. Studies in recent years have shown that identity is a complex phenomenon and religious affiliation often seems to be of crucial importance. This is to be seen, for example, in the World Council of Churches' (WCC's) discussions about unity within the community; similar discussions are taking place in the Anglican community when member churches sometimes have problems understanding that the work and decisions of other member churches are compatible with Christian or Anglican beliefs. Lutheran Churches are naturally not without challenges of this type. The purpose of this question is to examine the formation of the Lutheran tradition today in some churches that belong to the LWF. What role does the Lutheran tradition play in the theology and life of these churches?

The second question—How are churches affected by the globally growing Pentecostal or Charismatic influences—focuses on the rapid expansion of Evangelical, Fundamentalist and Charismatic movements around the world and their influence on other churches. The religious map of the world has changed dramatically in recent years. This has affected traditional churches (i.e., the Roman Catholic, Anglican, and Lutheran churches), especially in Africa and Latin America, and influenced their life and theology in various ways, not least by forcing them to relate to the newer movements more actively. What is happening in churches? Is it to be understood as a protest and, if so, against what and is the protest reasonable?

The third question—What is the situation for women? And what theology underpins their situation within the churches?—involves paying special attention to gender issues. Besides describing the situation for women, the goal will be to identify the theology that underpins their situation in a specific church, whether it is marked by inequality and subjugation or by equality and equal opportunity.

Finally, the fourth question—What can be said to be present-day "burning issues," and how are they a part of the formation and identity of the church?—entails focusing on such issues, collecting examples, and

---

4. The interview questions used are reproduced in the Appendix.

examining what different churches perceive as important problems or issues today.

Together, the answers to the four questions were intended to give a picture of the churches that reveals many aspects of how they understand themselves. The nature of the questions should divulge theology and reflections about praxis. These four questions should provide good opportunities of relating to other topics that can enrich the image. Other questions would no doubt have produced other answers, but the descriptions of each church would probably be much the same. These four topics, with the emphasis on the first, elucidate the churches' self-understanding from different perspectives. The question about Lutheranism highlights what the churches understand that to be and in what way they consider the Lutheran heritage important for them, how it affects decisions and actions. The question about the role of women discusses the church's self-understanding by taking power into account and by highlighting the relation between the traditional culture and Christian beliefs. The question about Charismatic influences does the same by discussing the relation between the denominational belief and other Christian beliefs. The question about burning issues probes what the churches see as their main challenges and how those challenges affect them.

However, while the first question was to be the main focus, it turned out that when informants were invited to answer questions about Lutheran identity, they rarely answered in identity terms. The answers tended to be vague and be more like deliberations or reflections in terms of burning issues. This has meant that when analyzing the material, it has been hard to find much about the construction of Lutheran identity. Another way of getting a grip on the Lutheran heritage and how it affects actions and decisions was therefore needed. This way involved analyzing how the churches are handling the dilemmas which are evident from their answers and to see how their Lutheran heritage interacts with or guides their decisions and actions in handling those dilemmas.

INTERVIEWS AND PAPERS

A study like this could of course be done from the office in Sweden, for example by means of a quantitative questionnaire survey or by using secondary material. However, that would probably have failed to throw light on important aspects.[5] The study aims to give the churches themselves a

---

5. See for example Kvale, *Den kvalitativa forskningsintervjun*.

hearing instead of simply relying on opinions or discussions about them. Moreover, a quantitative study would have been less capable of finding out about the current arguments, considerations and discussions in each church. It was therefore decided to do a qualitative study.[6]

One important way of gathering information for this study has been through interviews. Making interviews is a form of research that is appropriate when looking for answers that entail reasoning.[7] It is therefore suitable when looking for statements about a church that are nuanced and thoughtful. In each church, semi-structured interviews were held with between five and eight persons. Each interview lasted between approximately one and two hours and most interviews were done with one informant at a time; a few were done with a group. The informants had been chosen in advance by the church as having long and good knowledge of their church. This means that almost all the informants had belonged in some way to the church leadership. All interviews have been recorded.

No interviews were done with ordinary church-goers or active parishioners. Interviewing persons with no theological training or special responsibility in the church would no doubt have produced different answers but this was not done for various reasons. First, if just a few interviews are to be made in each church, it is important that each respondent can provide both correct and relevant information as well as some background. Second, the interviews were arranged by each church, which had an interest in picking persons with good knowledge, people they can "rely on." Thirdly and most importantly, this study is interested in each church's official self-reflection and therefore needed to use the churches' leadership as informants.

The interviews have been complemented with papers written by four researchers in each country. They were contacted either directly or through the church in question. Each researcher was given a topic to discuss in about ten to twenty pages. The topics were the same as the questions for the interviews: (1) How is Lutheran identity constructed today (in the church in question)? (2) How is the church (in question) affected by the globally growing Pentecostal or Charismatic influences? (3) What is the situation for women (in the church in question)? And what theology underpins their situation within the church? (4) What can be said to be present-day "burning issues" (in the church in question) and how are they a part of the

---

6. A relevant discussion of qualitative research is to be found in: Gubrium and Holstein, *New Language of Qualitative Method*.

7. Kvale, *Den kvalitativa forskningsintervjun*, 35–37, 81–82.

church's formation and identity? The researchers were then free to form their papers in their own way. This gave the material a scholarly aspect in addition to the interviews with church representatives. It should be noted, however, that the primary purpose of this was not to include a critical aspect of the churches but to provide a better picture. Even if the researchers were in theory independent of the churches, they were mostly in close connection and trusted by the church leaders. In a few cases it was, for various reasons, not possible to get a paper written. A seminar was arranged in each country at which the papers were presented and discussed, in some cases in co-operation with local educational institutions or church structures. When possible, services and other church gatherings were attended to supplement the other information.

The empirical material for this study was gathered during four trips in 2009–10 in which I was accompanied by Associate Professor Göran Gunner at the Church of Sweden Research Unit and, for one of them (Latin America), Associate Professor Anne-Louise Eriksson, who was then head of the Research Unit, and for another one (Iceland), Hanna Stenström, then at the Research Unit. The first church we visited was the ELCI in Iceland. This was to some extent a pilot study; Iceland's culture and the ELCI's folk church character are something with which I, as a Swedish researcher, feel familiar and therefore find easier to understand and see what does or does not work at interviews and other meetings. After a few minor adjustments, the other countries were visited. The visit to each church lasted for up to a week.

IMAGES OF THE CHURCHES

An image of each church has been constructed from the material. This image could of course have been made both deeper and broader by including facts and material from other studies, but the aim of this study has been to present the churches with the material they themselves provided, not by using secondary sources. It is their self-reflections that are in focus. The descriptions are therefore based entirely on the information obtained during our visits. In that way, the descriptions are a mixture of the information gathered by interviews in the churches and information gathered from the research papers and interviews with the researchers. The information given by the church is essentially the same as what the researchers provided. Their emphasis sometimes differs and sometimes the information from one source makes other information more understandable, but they never contradict each other.

This method for gathering and handling the information does not give an image of each church that is objective, free of errors or exaggerations. It gives the image that is presented by influential officials in each church. But even though the descriptions are built on a few influential informants, it is hoped that each image would be seen as relevant and understandable by other members in the church. The descriptions of the churches have therefore been read by at least one person from each church to see if they can "recognize" their church from the text. Those readings have led to some minor corrections of facts.

The structure of the images of the churches is not to be understood as answering the four questions directly. The four questions, with emphasis on the first, have instead primarily functioned as a way to get information that can form a more general image. The different informants from the different churches have answered the questions in different ways and put a different focus on them, depending on their particular situation. The images aim to reflect that in a relevant way; they endeavor to get a hold on what the informants are saying about their churches, rather than trying to answer the four questions directly. The four questions are primarily to be understood as a way to create larger images of the churches, not just as questions to be answered. It is therefore natural and important that the images of the churches are structured in different ways, have different headings and have their main focus on different subjects.

The descriptions contain footnotes to the papers used and to other material given to us. Moreover, everyone who was interviewed can be followed, by footnotes or by name, in the text.

SELF-REFLECTIONS

In this study I use the concept of self-reflection instead of identity. Identity has been an important and commonly discussed topic in various disciplines for at least fifty years. Political scientists have discussed the concept of identity in relation to violence, immigration and many other issues. In sociology, social anthropology, and other academic disciplines the concept of identity has played important roles. Similarly, identity is an important concept in the field of theology, used in a wide variety of ways, for instance to explain or problematize religious experiences or expressions in history and today.[8]

An important theological or ecclesiological understanding of the concept identity that relates to this study is to be found in Professor Johannes van der Ven's book *Ecclesiology in Context*.[9] In his attempt to come to grips with the identity of a church, he uses two concepts: basis and identity and states that ". . . the *basis* has to do with the relationship of the church to the Christian tradition."[10] This makes the basis very decisive for the church. To be Catholic, Lutheran, or Calvinistic are examples of churches' basis. He then adds that ". . . the possible change of this basis can be seen as the most decisive matter in which the local church can involve itself. It touches upon its very foundation."[11] While the basis of a church may be very difficult to change, ". . . the identity is not set, but changes together with the historical and societal context in which the church finds itself."[12] In van der Ven's construction, identity is made up of four components: context, convictions, vision, and mission. The four interact and affect each other in a circular or spiral way. The context is about the social realities—in a broad sense—in which a church finds itself. Convictions answer the question: What do we believe? Vision is to some extent built on the former and answers the question: Who are we? Mission, finally, is about the task of the church: What are we striving for?[13]

Other well-known examples of theories concerning identity in relation to churches are constructed by Don Browning and Thomas Groome. Both of them have constructed ways to describe congregations and relate those descriptions to historical and systematic theology as ways to understand and develop what is happening in the congregations.[14]

However, what I am doing in this study does not have to do with using the concept of identity in the above-mentioned ways. The study does not test a sociological or empirical theory, neither on group nor individual level, but tries to do justice to the church leaders' theoretical reflections

---

8. Roth, *Identitet och pluralism*.

9. van der Ven, *Ecclesiology in Context*, 151–52.

10. Ibid., 151.

11. Ibid.

12. Ibid., 152.

13. Ibid.

14. See for example: Browning, *Fundamental Practical Theology*; Groome, *Way of Shared Praxis*.

about their churches, their self-reflections. These self-reflections make up a picture of how they are talking about who they are, why they act as they do and why certain decisions are made. What this study is trying to doing is not to pin down objectively controllable facts about each church, but to do justice to how church leaders describe their churches, joys and difficulties. Starting from these descriptions, it is possible to discuss how the Lutheran heritage is used in handling dilemmas.

STRUCTURE AND PURPOSE

The book consists of five chapters. The first chapter discusses the background to the study's main question. Although the Church of Sweden is a Lutheran church by confession and self-understanding—and has been so for centuries—the Lutheran heritage is constantly debated: What does being a Lutheran church mean today? And how does it affect the church's decisions and actions? Other Lutheran churches are probably also struggling with the same questions in a similar way.

The next chapter discusses the study's questions and the method chosen. The issues include the selection of countries and churches, how the material has been analyzed and the study's structure.

Chapter three presents the five selected churches: the ILCO in Costa Rica, the IECLB in Brazil, the ELCI in Iceland, the FLM in Madagascar, and the HKBP in Indonesia. The descriptions are based on interviews with church leaders and research papers written in each country. The description of each church should be understood, not as a critical assessment but as a report on how the leaders of that church reflect on their church.

In the fourth chapter the empirical material is subjected to a systematic theological discussion. From the presentations in chapter three it is evident that all five churches are dealing with some dilemmas, dilemmas that are often discussed in systematic theology. In dealing with these dilemmas, the churches act in different ways, depending on history, context and other factors. When the descriptions of the churches are related to a systematic theological discussion, it is possible to see what the churches understand as important.

The fifth chapter discusses what the churches activate in terms of their Lutheran tradition when trying to handle the dilemmas they face. What seems to be important for them to accomplish and what "Lutheran tools" do they use for this? The chapter ends in a general discussion about the study's outcome and considers a few challenges this poses for Lutheran churches around the globe.

This study aims both to provide a picture of how church leaders describe five Lutheran churches and to discuss how Lutheranism is understood and used in handling dilemmas confronting the churches, and thereby contribute to Lutheran churches' reflections on their Lutheran heritage. The hope is that this will enhance the possibilities for churches to learn from each other. Another hope is that the study will contribute to a broader understanding of the challenges facing the LWF family and thereby not only provide a possibility of learning from each other but also lead to deeper theological reflection. It is also important to say that the study does not aim to compare the different churches with each other or with a "correct" image of the Lutheran tradition. The churches in this study *are* Lutheran in their self-understanding and through membership of the LWF and the aim is to see and discuss what is seen, not to criticize and correct. My hope is that this book can be used as a means of getting a perspective, not only on the churches presented here, but also on a wider front.

SOME ETHICAL CONSIDERATIONS

All churches in the study were asked to take part well in advance by letter or e-mail and were also given the possibility of declining. Individuals involved in some way as informants were contacted in advance by their church and given the four questions to be discussed. As to confidentiality, nothing has been concealed. The names of countries, churches and informants are open and this was communicated to the informants. An alternative could of course have been to have everything anonymous but that would have made it hard to present the churches in a meaningful way. Yet another alternative could have been not to disclose the names of the informants but have the names of the countries and churches open. However, most of the informants are high-ranking officials in their respective church, and it is important for the reader to know for sure who says what.

3

Five Churches

This chapter presents the five churches.[1] They have different backgrounds and different histories, but are all struggling with how to be a true church at that place and time. They all understand themselves as Lutheran churches.

COSTA RICA—IGLESIA LUTHERANA COSTARRICENSE, ILCO

Between Panama and Nicaragua there is a small, but in many ways rich, country—Costa Rica.[2] The name presumably indicates how the country was perceived when Columbus landed there in 1502. In that case, it did not live up to expectations. There was no gold or other minerals, the land was difficult to cultivate and the native population, already small at that time, was decimated by the diseases which Europeans brought with them. All this resulted in Costa Rica remaining a poor country far away from the regional center in Guatemala, and mainly populated by Spanish descendants working on small family farms. However, the relative poverty proved to be a blessing: Costa Rica was able to develop gradually in its own way, largely without either external interference or major divisive internal fractions. The numerous small farms, so different from the often vast haciendas in

---

1. The text is mainly built on interviews and unprinted sources. The interviews are marked "interviews" in the footnotes and the informants' names are given in the footnotes. The informants are listed in the bibliography under the heading "Interviews". The unprinted sources are marked "UP" in the footnotes and are listed in the bibliography under the heading "Unprinted sources".

2. The brief introductions to the countries are not footnoted. The information there is general knowledge, easily accessed in any guidebook.

the wealthier neighboring countries, paved the way for development and democracy.

Today, Costa Rica is a stable democracy in relatively unstable surroundings. Besides being unstable, the region has a reputation for violence. In Nicaragua, the Sandinistas overthrew the Somoza dictatorship in 1979, after which a civil war raged for almost a decade. Other neighboring countries, such as El Salvador, Guatemala, and Honduras, were military dictatorships for many years in the twentieth century. So, Costa Rica is the region's exception. A democracy since 1889 with a law from 1949 that prohibits an army. Education has been free for everyone since 1869, though children from poorer families tend to leave school after six years. The legal system is well developed and the media are protected, at least in theory, from political intervention. Thus, Costa Rica differs from its neighbors in many respects.

Costa Rica is known as a beautiful country with rain forests, volcanoes and biological diversity, hosting five percent of the Earth's species. The pillars of the economy are agricultural products—primarily bananas—tourism and electronics. At the same time, there are huge gaps between the richest and the poorest; illegal immigrants—mostly from Nicaragua—experience a difficult situation; society is patriarchal and women traditionally take second place, though that is now changing; most of the indigenous population lives in remote rural areas. Costa Rica, like all societies, is a mixture of good and bad, high and low, the country where today's Costa Ricans or "ticos" live.

This also is now a country with a Lutheran church, Iglesia Lutherana Costarricense (ILCO).

Being a Sign of Hope

The ILCO was founded as recently as 1988, not as a result of missionary activity from abroad, but by Costa Ricans who, for various reasons, felt out of place in other churches. It likes to be known as a church for people who are "not welcome" in other churches, and a church rooted in its praxis.

> [The ILCO is a church] for people who are uprooted in different aspects of human experience, be it due to immigration, or as in my case, frustration with alternative Christian religious groups; this space offers a place of basic solidarity and spirituality, absent on the Costa Rican scene. Spiritual movement means that it is a

group that freely gathers in order to live something meaningful; the praxis is the core of the spiritual life, not confession or dogma.³

The ILCO is a small church. There is no register of members, but they say that probably 5000 people are involved in the ILCO's work in various ways. The reason for not registering members is theological; according to missionary Katarina Hedqvist, the ILCO wants to be seen as ecumenical and a salt in the world, rather than a proselytizing church.⁴ It is present in twenty-five places spread all over the country. Some function as real congregations with pastoral work and church services, others are places where the ILCO's work is to be found on a less regular basis.⁵ An important aspect of the ILCO's self-understanding is that the church is made visible not just as a worshiping community but also—and perhaps mainly—in its actions in society at large. Sometimes Luke 4:18 is seen as presenting the ILCO's core vision: "The Spirit of the Lord is upon me, because he has anointed me to bring good news to the poor. He has sent me to proclaim release to the captives and recovery of sight to the blind, to let the oppressed go free."⁶ For a church to be incarnate it has to take form in society, according to the ILCO. For the ILCO that means it has to take form among the poor. Poverty refers here to more than economic poverty, though of course that often accompanies other forms of poverty. Poverty can mean many different things where people have been deprived of their rights and dignity. But it is also interesting to note that one reason for ILCO's relatively strong voice is that some poor groups have more of a voice in society than others. For instance, an economically poor person is less likely to have a better education and a good job than a person who is poor in terms of being excluded because of sexual orientation. Both groups have a place in the ILCO. But, of course, many people belong to more than one poverty group, for instance those who are both homosexual and economically poor.

The ILCO's present—and first—bishop, Melwin Jiménez, summarizes the church's task in this way: "[w]ith the background in our faith in Christ, together with vulnerable groups in both urban settings and the countryside, [we should] contribute to worship, brotherhood and reconciliation, based on these people's respective struggles and hopes." By letting one's faith have consequences, by sharing the sacraments, both individuals and

3. Mena Oreamuno, "ILCO: Spiritual Movement in a Symbiotic Culture," 10. UP.
4. Hedqvist, Katarina. Interview.
5. "Den costaricanska lutherska kyrkan." UP.
6. Hedqvist, "ILCO (Iglesia Lutherana Cosraricense)," 1. UP.

the church at large are called into a prophetic work for justice, love and solidarity; together with the poor they can be a sign of God's kingdom.[7] Bishop Melwin also says that the ILCO has opened up Pandora's box in Costa Rica and thereby raised a lot of very difficult questions that cannot be locked up again.[8] It is in this environment, with issues that tend to be ignored in the rest of society and together with people who seldom have the ability to speak for themselves, that the ILCO should work and be a sign of God. And being a sign of God's kingdom, not just in words, but in a really practical way, is important in the ILCO.

> Being a sign of hope in the middle of the patriarchal culture and of inhuman capitalism is a challenge that touches the deepest fibers of the Gospel and implies questioning not only economic and social structures, but also common and personal attitudes.
>
> The Costa Rican Lutheran Church (ILCO) has articulated an alternative message for more than twenty years. An alternative to the soporific and conservative speeches that some other churches preach, turning their messages into accomplices of the system, favoring people's resignation and passiveness, silencing the Gospel's constant cry on behalf of the Kingdom of God.[9]

Besides being a sign, it is important to be a movement. The members seem to use the word movement to describe the ILCO just as often as they use the word church. There are numerous reasons for this. Perhaps the most obvious one is that the ILCO has existed for only twenty-five years and was started in 1988 not as a church but as a small-scale movement with a few participants who wanted to be active in making a better world. It has now become a church with work spread all over Costa Rica. Today the ILCO is a member of the LWF with a bishop as its leader, but it still has its roots in a movement and in many ways still understands itself as such. Moreover, this is how it is often seen by others.[10] Second, the ILCO's theology has its point of departure in the theology of liberation. The center is not theology in the form of dogma but rather theology in the form of praxis. To be, or to understand itself as a movement is important and opens up for forms of behavior that are "unorthodox." Pastor Gilberto Quesada Mora expresses it in this way:

7. Ibid.
8. Jiménez, Melwin. Interview.
9. Rojas Campell, "A Spirit that Frees from the Closet," 1. UP.
10. Hedqvist, Magnus. Interview.

> It is a crazy church, this one, in the sense of going against the mainstream. When I'm at meetings with representatives from other churches I can't help asking myself, "is it they who are crazy or us?" But my answer is that every church has something on which it focuses its attention. I think that the most important thing for our continuing to be like this is that we are a movement. It opens up for us to be a heretical church. Heretical in the sense that we dare to call everything by its proper name, we don't hide things. We are a church that dares to speak up when it is needed.[11]

From the nature of the church as a movement it follows that the ILCO has no problem working together with other movements or NGOs (Non-Governmental Organizations) even if they do not have a Christian foundation. What matters for the ILCO is the practical work. If an NGO in its praxis works for the realization of God's kingdom on earth, it will make a good partner for the ILCO. By establishing bonds with other organizations and working together for a better world, the ILCO sees itself as having a prophetic voice in society as a church.[12] Today, at least forty NGOs have some kind of partnership with the ILCO in its work on, for instance, renegotiation of the free trade agreement (FTA) with the USA, immigration laws, laws concerning the independence of the indigenous population, campaigns against HIV, work for labor rights and environmental concerns at the fruit plantations, and laws concerning domestic violence.[13] People are not used to seeing or hearing churches struggle with what can be understood as political topics and they are certainly not used to seeing them work together with non-church organizations, according to Gilberto Quesada Mora.

> Suddenly, those who are out demonstrating on the streets meet the church in the same demonstration. People are not used to that. They see that we are involved in the same struggle as they are. That is a great experience for many. They can see God in a different way from before.[14]

---

11. Quesada Mora, Gilberto. Interview.
12. Ibid.
13. Hedqvist, "ILCO (Iglesia Lutherana Cosraricense)," 2. UP.
14. Quesada Mora, Gilberto. Interview.

A Church without Walls

A common saying in the ILCO is that it would like to be a church without walls. That is, a church open for everyone, with interlocutors in different parts of society; a church that wants to cooperate with different parts of society regardless of faith and confession. One could say that the creation of the ILCO was not a matter of a church searching for a mission, but a mission searching for a church.[15] In its activities, the ILCO has three general purposes:

- To stimulate and promote the proclamation of the Bible and the administration of the sacraments in accordance with the Lutheran confession.

- To actively take part in evangelizing activities, which include education, development and emergency work, in a way that reflects the holistic view of man which the Bible teaches.

- To participate in ecumenical dialogues and take part in joint programs both with other churches and with other national and international bodies that help to create a fairer society and a more peaceful world.[16]

This radical openness is founded on the fact that the ILCO's members often understand or talk about the church as if it has a mission for the whole person, not just for the soul.[17] They mean that by emphasizing body and soul, not as a dichotomy but as an inseparable unit, they understand God's creation more correctly and fully than churches which only emphasize a spiritual salvation. The Gospel is only the Gospel if it really means changes for the poor. Pastor Carlos Bonilla says, "[w]hat I like most is the social commitment. Most churches distinguish the political from the religious; in the ILCO we try to hold them together."[18] Therefore, an important mission for the ILCO is to constantly make visible the links between the Gospel and the context in which it is preached.[19] To be a church without walls is one way to try to "live" that vision.

> The articulation of the ILCO with organizations that fight for human rights, ensuring the protection of human dignity and unmasking the interests of the powerful ones in the system. This

15. Hedqvist, "Missionärsrapportering från Costa Rica," 3. UP.
16. "Den costaricanska lutherska kyrkan," 1. UP.
17. Quesada Mora, Gilberto. Interview.
18. Bonilla, Carlos. Interview.
19. Hedqvist, "ILCO (Iglesia Lutherana Cosraricense)," 2. UP.

action has implied a permanent dialogue with civil society and the establishment of networks and alliances "to walk together" in topics of national interest. Very few churches or religious groups assume this commitment to the environment.

The role and presence of the ILCO have allowed it to be close and take the lead in some topics considered uncomfortable not only in the churches but also in other conservative parts of society: gender, sexuality, sexual diversity and legal abortion are considered taboo in our culture, where ignorance and distortion are created by conservative groups and require true internal reflection and responsible debate.[20]

This enables the church to work together with other actors; moreover, the commitment to work together with poor people and with questions that the majority society often sees as non-questions has influenced the ILCO's organizational structure. Over the years, the structure and the working focus have developed to what they are today, but the main focus has always been on preaching the Word, administering the sacraments, and serving society on the basis of a holistic view of creation. Today, the ILCO's work is divided into three parts. First there are the real church communities with a priest in charge and a more strict work and organization; there are eleven such places. The other two parts could be characterized both as places for pastoral work and legal aid work where services are held more irregularly, and as activities for supporting a certain need in an area or among a group of people.[21]

One example of the way the ILCO works in its congregations is Alajuelita. This is a very poor part of the capital San José where most of the 5000 inhabitants are marginalized in some way. Crime, drug abuse, violence, and prostitution are common in their daily lives. A large proportion have a background in neighboring countries, for instance El Salvador and Nicaragua. Basic needs in a normal society—water supplies, schools, electricity—are non-existent. The ILCO has been present in Alajuelita since 1994 and is now a well-functioning congregation. It all started with the ILCO, together with a local committee, providing legal aid for poor families so that they could build a home on a piece of land of their own. The work was then extended to include, for example, a preschool for children of single parents and free medical care for women. The latter is done in collaboration with an NGO. The ILCO also works on helping immigrants find

20. Rojas Campell, "A Spirit that Frees from the Closet," 2. UP.
21. "Den costaricanska lutherska kyrkan," 1–11. UP.

a place in Costa Rica. Another activity is a group which teaches the younger generation folk dances from Costa Rica and Nicaragua.[22]

As mentioned above, there are also places for pastoral work and legal aid work where services are held less regularly. One example is Paleque el Sol, a community made up of families from the indigenous Maleku people. They total approximately 600 persons living in a very poor part of northern Costa Rica. The ILCO started to work there in 1993, first with legal aid and then, from 2000, with a church community. Core activities are work with children and education for women. There are also bible studies, pastoral counseling, and services. In 2005, with help from two American church groups, they built a parish house that the municipality uses as a school. An important aspect of the work involves strengthening cultural traditions that have largely been forgotten.[23]

Furthermore, the ILCO is involved in a wide variety of projects and with work in different committees; examples are assistance for victims of natural disasters and support for immigrants. There are seven committees, each responsible for a particular segment of the ILCO's work, for instance leadership training, planning, and evaluation. Today there are committees for women, children, youth, indigenous people, immigrants, church relations, HIV/AIDS-related issues, and issues concerning HBT and, in particular, transgender people (the Committee for Diversity).[24]

The ILCO has been successful in many ways. Although relatively small, it is an important factor in Costa Rican society. It has widespread connections both in society and with NGOs. It is also a profound voice in public debates about the wellbeing of the poor in Costa Rica. But while it does have a public presence, the ILCO also sees itself as a loner among the churches. Church member Christina Mora puts it like this: "I think of the ILCO as being like the people of Israel in ancient times. Just like them, we are surrounded by big religious empires that want to silence us. But nevertheless we, like Israel, have a strong voice."[25] To be a church without walls is important for the ILCO but it has also left the church alone in its corner among fellow churches.

22. Ibid., 2.
23. Ibid., 6.
24. Ibid., 7–11.
25. Mora, Christina. Interview.

The Religious Context

The religious milieu in Costa Rica is historically Catholic; article 75 in the Constitution states that the Catholic belief is the belief of the State. There were hardly any other churches until the mid-1980s, when various Evangelical churches started to spread over the country and grow more rapidly. The common perception was that Evangelical or Neo-Pentecostal churches would soon have a majority but this has not happened. Evangelical churches are certainly growing but instead of changing churches, people are mainly losing interest in religion. Commitment to a faith or a church is weakening. People are attracted to what is new and interesting but do not stay.[26]

> Evangelicals/Protestants have huge churches with specialized shows. While these churches are full of people in almost every service, the fact is that people just pass through. They don't stay, and they don't have the same commitment as they did 15 years ago.[27]

Even so, people do still come into contact with Evangelical churches and evangelical theology in various ways, not least frequent TV shows, etc. What they encounter is churches where "[t]he focus is spiritual warfare and prosperity. There is no reference to the discipleship of Christ or his practice, or his faith, or any of the main issues that constitute the core of Christian faith."[28] This is a huge problem on a general level, according to the ILCO, but does not seem to be a major practical problem. To understand why this is not a problem it should be remembered that the ILCO is rooted in its praxis, not its dogma. Gilberto Quesada Mora explains this by saying:

> I have never seen this as a problem. For us it is natural that our parishes are mixtures of Catholics, Neo-Pentecostals, Lutherans and so on. We are living in a praxis that is ecumenical. We never distinguish between people; this has to do with our identity, being open.[29]

While the Evangelical churches are the most vocal, the Catholic Church is by far the largest. It is also a very powerful institution, not least politically.[30] But even the Catholic Church is in decline. It still has a huge impact on society but people are tending to do more and more without

26. Mena Oreamuno, "ILCO: Spiritual Movement in a Symbiotic Culture," 6. UP.
27. Ibid., 7.
28. Ibid.
29. Quesada Mora, Gilberto. Interview.
30. Hedqvist, Magnus. Interview.

consulting the church. It is, for instance, increasingly difficult for the Catholic Church to find persons with a priestly vocation. Another example is that people are becoming less inclined to involve the church in family events; for example, in 2008 church weddings were used for only 21 percent of all marriages.[31] The basic trend in Costa Rica seems to be for people to lose confidence in political structures and also in churches. Even so, Costa Rica is a Catholic country officially and the Catholic Church still has a huge influence on people's values.

In this setting, with an established Catholic church that is conservative, especially when it comes to family values, and with equally conservative and also highly vocal Evangelical or Neo-Pentecostal churches, the ILCO stresses its message of being a church without walls, working together with the poor. That is a message which is seldom accepted by or in line with either other churches or conservative elements in society. This situation—with a predominantly conservative society as well as theologically and ethically conservative churches that are numerically large and have strong voices, even though they seem to be in decline—has resulted in the ILCO having a very specific role in debates, the media and society in general.

Researcher Miguel Rojas Campell writes that a fundamental challenge for the church in this kind of situation is to transmit an alternative reflection on God, instead of what other churches normally present.[32] A common opinion among the ILCO's members is that the country's other churches mainly support a very conservative theology that makes little sense as a means of liberating people from what is holding them down. Bishop Melwin expresses this by saying, "[b]oth a Catholic priest and an Evangelical pastor say 'I have the truth', when they pick up their Bible. We say 'let us explore together'. That makes a very different church."[33] Christina Mora says she thinks other churches regard the ILCO as a church that does not take responsibility for people's souls.[34] But they do, church official Xinia Chacon says; they take responsibility both for peoples' souls and for their bodies. They see to people's lives here and now.[35]

---

31. Mena Oreamuno, "ILCO: Spiritual Movement in a Symbiotic Culture," 7. UP.
32. Rojas Campell, "A Spirit that Frees from the Closet," 3. UP.
33. Jiménez, Melwin. Interview.
34. Mora, Christina. Interview.
35. Chacón, Xinia. Interview.

According to Miguel Rojas Campell, many of the ideas about God that other churches propagate affect people's lives in many ways and make them feel they don't deserve anything better. The way things are is God's will; God does not want change. He mentions some themes which he sees as important for the ILCO to oppose. One is the perception of God as omnipresent. Others are that God is associated with power, obedience and punishment, and that God is distant. He also points to the lack of communication between God and humans; God is silent and only speaks through "worthy" people, a category to which the poor do not belong. God is also distant to the reality of the body and human sexuality. God is the God of purity.[36]

Most of the people the ILCO encounters, in various settings, live with this type of theology. People who, for example, are gay, lesbian, divorced, or have a sexual life outside marriage, live with shame and fear; they think of themselves as unworthy and justly excluded from rights.[37] Francisco Mena Oreamuno talks about what he sees as a lack of theological thinking in Coast Rica. Neither the Catholic Church nor the Evangelical churches have a living theological discussion. He adds that "[t]he only serious formal theological background is that which comes from Latin American Liberation Theology and it has been satanized by both groups."[38] A paper by missionaries Katarina and Magnus Hedqvist states that in Costa Rica, as in many other countries, most churches proclaim a message that contradicts the message of the ILCO and instead separates religion from politics, body from soul, etc.[39]

Women's Situation

Costa Rica is a patriarchal society and women's situation has been on the ILCO's agenda right from the start. According to Christina Mora, many groups in the country are experiencing a troublesome time and in all of them it is women who are at the bottom of the hierarchy.[40] The ILCO therefore strives to strengthen the situation of women in various ways. One is to participate in public debate in society in general; another is to work with its own church organization so that obstacles for women's participation are sorted out. In practice, both the outward and the inward activities can

---

36. Rojas Campell, "A Spirit that Frees from the Closet," 4. UP.
37. Ibid., 6.
38. Mena Oreamuno, "ILCO: Spiritual Movement in a Symbiotic Culture," 11. UP.
39. Hedqvist, "ILCO (Iglesia Lutherana Cosraricense)," 2. UP.
40. Mora, Christina. Interview.

involve education, encouraging women to take leading positions, and actions against violence and economic inequality.[41]

Christina Mora point out that most people in the ILCO are women and they are also more active in church matters than men. Women in the ILCO also say they feel that men listen to them and they have no problem stating their opinion in discussions. Especially compared with the rest of society, they think the ILCO is a good place when it comes to equality between men and women. Christina Mora says:

> We are more active than men, we talk more, and we participate more. We do everything more as long as it concerns the church. As soon as the subject moves away to other matters outside the church we are silent and find it much harder to talk. But that is not because of the ILCO, it is cultural.[42]

Men confirm this by saying that the situation is much better in the ILCO than in society in general, but there is still some way to go before they achieve total equality in the church.[43] Today there are no Costa Rican women pastors in the ILCO. Bishop Melwin explains the situation in terms of the social situation: "There are women today who are studying theology with a view to being ordained. But they need a lot of help and support if they are going to reach their goal. Today women in Costa Rica do not have the same opportunities as men, economically and socially."[44] He goes on to say that in some way the ILCO is trapped by the LWF's regulations, which stipulate that anyone who is going to be ordained must have a university degree. It makes no difference if you come from a rich or a poor country. Consequently it is very hard to find people who qualify for theological training and even harder to find women. If we altered the regulations and ordained people with a shorter education, the wealthier churches would probably look on us as a second-class church. There will be women pastors from Costa Rica but it will take time.[45]

As to society, the ILCO states that women are almost always the biggest losers, not least economically or from being beaten by their husbands. Therefore the ILCO has for many years done a huge work among women, both in the larger cities and in small villages in rural areas. A main purpose

41. "Den costaricanska lutherska kyrkan," 8–11. UP.
42. Mora, Christina. Interview.
43. Quesada Mora, Gilberto. Interview.
44. Jiménez, Melwin. Interview.
45. Ibid.

is to strengthen women and restore their dignity, but also to help them earn an income.⁴⁶ Bishop Melwin explains:

> I have no statistics to show whether their economic situation has improved but it is clear to me that in twenty years' time many women will be engaged in our church in various ways and take their commitment with them to places outside the church. They have their own voice.⁴⁷

Most work is done in small villages in rural areas. It often begins with an invitation to women to a gathering to discuss how handicraft or something similar could help improve their economy. After some time, discussions often also include situations at home. Dignity, human rights, violence, and sexuality are not always easy to talk about and the work must be seen as a long-term effort; but according to the ILCO this type of work is important, first of all for women, but also for society in general. In this kind of work it is equally important, but even more difficult, to discuss the same subjects with the women's husbands, fathers, brothers etc. It is not only women who need support; men are victims too, just by living in a patriarchal society, according to the ILCO. Therefore this type of work must be understood as a complex matter with different layers.⁴⁸ Women's situation has been an important field of work in the ILCO since the church was founded in 1988. A special women's group was started in 1994 and in 2005 this group was turned into a formal committee with representatives from every district where the ILCO is to be found.⁴⁹

Leadership

In the general structure of the ILCO, every parish has, or should have, a parish board. At national level there is a church synod that meets every second or third year. In theory the church synod is the highest body for decisions in the church but in praxis—partly because of the long interval between its meetings—that role is performed by the church board.⁵⁰

Today the ILCO has an ordained bishop. The first and current bishop, Melwin Jiménez, was ordained on April 27, 2008, at a solemn service

---

46. Ibid.
47. Ibid.
48. "Kyrkan som vill stå på Livets sida," 1. UP.
49. "Den costaricanska lutherska kyrkan," 8. UP.
50. Hedqvist, "Missionärsrapportering från Costa Rica," 4. UP.

attended by representatives from other churches. The decision to appoint a bishop was deliberated during the ILCO's first twenty years and was not self-evident. As a church with a background in a "movement," the change was quite a big step. However, Melwin Jiménez has proved to be a person with good leadership qualities and when the media started to refer to him as "Bishop," the church board decided it was time to adopt that title instead of chairman. There were some who deplored what they saw as a lack of a prior theological discussion and the parishes were never involved in the decision, which was made by the church board, where three of the ILCO's founders were still members. In a way, the change from chairman to bishop shows that the ILCO is a very pragmatic church.[51] If something is good for it or is seen as the best way to express God's will, it is done. Today the decision has solid support in the church.[52] Bishop Melwin describes the situation and his role by saying:

> In all movements there has to be someone who goes first, enthuses others and makes them willing to come along. If there is no such person, nothing will happen. That is how I see my role in this church. Some find it a problem that I am not seen that often. But I think it is a strong point that I can let other people be in charge. I can leave decisions to others. In my opinion, the different groups are functioning very well. Other people lead them and do the work. For me it is enough to be informed. When I go to other churches I can see that the bishop is everywhere. I am not. It is important to have a movement where people have confidence in each other.[53]

When it comes to how the church reacts when opinions differ on a particular question, a common view is that the ILCO's foundation is its praxis, not its belief or dogma. Those who would like to take a stand for the poor and exploited stay in the church, while those who are looking for a different type of church move away.[54] Others say that issues about democracy and leadership in the church are issues with which the church is struggling and will have to struggle even more in the future. They say that if the ILCO is to be a church without walls, it must solve the question of who is allowed to say something about the church and be listened to. Who are in and who

51. Ibid., 4–5.
52. Ibid., 5.
53. Jiménez, Melwin. Interview.
54. Quesada Mora, Gilberto. Interview.

are out? How can the ILCO give a voice to those who are on the margin of the church—and will it do that? For whom will the ILCO be a voice?[55] Another important factor about the ILCO's leadership and openness could be what Francisco Mena Oreamuno says must be born in mind, namely that the leaders themselves come from backgrounds that taught them what it is like to be without power, without a voice.

> The leadership of the ILCO is constituted by people who come from diverse institutional religious experiences in which they didn't find space, because of their theological position or life histories. They aren't Lutheran by tradition, but rather excluded and marginalized from their original religious experiences.[56]

The ILCO is financially poor; 80 percent of its funds come from other Lutheran churches, mainly in Germany, the USA and Sweden. The range of contributors means that the ILCO is not bound to a specific church, country or culture, according to Katarina Hedqvist.[57]

Theological Foundations

The ILCO is not a church of writing; it is a church of practice. And the practice is founded in the Word, the Sacraments and in servanthood.[58] What this means can be summarized as "My actions are my words."[59] Similarly, Bishop Melwin says that theology is reflection about life and it is therefore issues concerning life that are in the foreground—not theology. Or as Francisco Mena Oreamuno puts it, "[p]astoral ministry is the heart of the identity of the ILCO—everything else comes after that, its reflection, its message and kerygma."[60] But even if practice is the first step and theology the second, theological formation, to shape, create, maintain, build and assert a Lutheran identity, is also important in the ILCO.[61] Not least, theology provides tools for guiding the church in its practice.

> To assert one's identity is to build one's history; to make history. And one's identity is nurtured, sustained and asserted in times of

---

55. Hedqvist, "Missionärsrapportering från Costa Rica," 5. UP.
56. Mena Oreamuno, "ILCO: Spiritual Movement in a Symbiotic Culture," 10. UP.
57. Hedqvist, Katarina. Interview.
58. Bonilla, Carlos. Interview.
59. Mena Oreamuno, "ILCO: Spiritual Movement in a Symbiotic Culture," 12. UP.
60. Ibid., 13.
61. Gierus, "Joint Research Project," 3. UP.

crisis, in situations of social struggle, in our daily life struggles. The construction of the ILCO's identity is closely linked to social activities that aim at obtaining sustainability and self-management, not just financial. The Lutheran formation and biblico-theological reflections are necessary aids in providing support for this identity.[62]

Bishop Melwin also stresses the importance of Lutheran theology for identity. He points to the importance of grace but also of the Bible for the church. And not just at its importance but also that every person has the right to work with it without the church correcting what people see in it.[63] The ILCO is a twenty-five-year-old Lutheran church but it is not a Lutheran church in the same sense as most other Lutheran churches in Europe or Latin America. As mentioned earlier, the ILCO is not a result of foreign missionary activity; it is profoundly Costa Rican or Latin American. So its relation to Luther and Lutheranism differs from that of most churches with a European foundation. To be a Lutheran in Costa Rica means being a mix of different things, being open for that mix and also being prepared to reformulate what was once said.[64]

> If I am ever heard, it will be with my Latin American and Costa Rican voice, not because I tried to learn a word that is foreign to me. We must develop a Lutheran catechism from Latin America with our own words and thoughts, then understand the European Lutheran catechism and only then see if they have something in common. Being Lutheran would in my opinion be to incorporate the principle of the Reformation in my own words: One faith (to be a spiritual movement rather than a religious institution), One Word (read our foundational texts from my own cultural experience), Universal priesthood (reinvent the community of faith in symmetrical relationships).

Therefore the experience of Luther and other voices of the Radical Reformation, such as Müntzer, will only be possible if we can connect from the depths of our love of life in God. Neither the creed nor the theology, neither the liturgy nor the name, but the life of faith, a life faithful to God, a life that expresses the freely given love of God—that will be the common ground which joins us to the worldwide Lutheran family. I can say, therefore, that the ILCO is re-creating Luther and making a contribution

---

62. Ibid., 4.
63. Jiménez, Melwin. Interview.
64. Quesada Mora, Gilberto. Interview.

to Lutheranism. What is needed is time to think it through and write about it.[65]

Gilberto Quesada Mora expresses the same by saying that we often think of Lutheran identity as Luther's identity. Instead of trying to grasp that, we have to go back to the intention of the Reformation and be a church that is in constant reformation. For the ILCO, that means to be a church that answers in the best way when people or creation cry for help.[66] It cannot get stuck in its form or other things if they are obstacles to helping create God's kingdom. Carlos Bonilla says that for him, Lutheran identity is two things. First it is reliance on a loving God, second it is trust that we have the ability and also God's approval to liberate us to become what God wants us to be. We are responsible for this world. What will come is already accomplished by Christ, but we have the responsibility for this world. Orthopraxy is better than orthodoxy.[67]

An expression often used in the ILCO is "another world is possible" but the expression "another church is possible" is also important. The church cannot stay the way it is without changing. It is of great importance that the church does not take itself for granted. Is it on the right track or does it need to change to become what it is meant to be? Every church lives in danger of being self-sufficient. Reformation is constantly needed.[68] The ILCO is a reformed church that has understood the importance of constant reformation, as Gilberto Quesada Mora says.[69]

Summary

The ILCO is in many ways an unusual church. First it is very small, just a thousand or so members, though it does have an impact on Costa Rican society in general that is out of proportion to its size. But first and foremost, the ILCO is unusual in its work among poor, marginalized and exploited people. It is a church that in many ways must be said to be directed outwardly more than inwardly. Members say that the ILCO strives to be a sign of God's kingdom in a practical way. They do this by trying not to separate the political from the religious. They are a church with a clear vision that God's kingdom is to be found not only in the small group but in society at

65. Mena Oreamuno, "ILCO: Spiritual Movement in a Symbiotic Culture," 12. UP.
66. Mora, Christina. Interview.
67. Bonilla, Carlos. Interview.
68. Hedqvist, "ILCO (Iglesia Lutherana Cosraricense)," 3. UP.
69. Quesada Mora, Gilberto. Interview.

large. While they try to "reach out," they would also like to be a church with a clear and stable center but the combination is not always easy to achieve.

Costa Rican society is essentially Catholic. It is a male-dominated country and one where groups such as immigrants, homosexuals, indigenous people and so on are in a very difficult situation. In that setting the ILCO tries to be an alternative to the major culture, an alternative that opens up possibilities for those who do not fit into the major culture. By being such an alternative they also try to open up the minds of people to alternative ways of understanding the gospel.

Renewal can be said to be an important word in the ILCO. The gospel should sound differently from what it used to sound; not that the traditional sound is mostly wrong, but that, according to ILCO, parts of human existence have been left out. They are trying to find new ways to reach people who have seldom been reached before but in doing that they also try to use the tradition in a way that answers present situations and questions. But it can also be said that tradition in the ILCO is weak. The church is very young, born out of a "movement," and therefore does not have much of a tradition to fall back on.

An important way in which the ILCO would like to describe itself is as "a church without walls." According to its members, traditional churches in Costa Rica are very homogeneous and large sections of the population are left out or seen, not as members of the church but as "working material." The ILCO has tried to find a way to create a church that is truly open at the same time as its center is stable.

The major tasks for the ILCO have been to give a voice to the voiceless, power to the powerless and so on, in an attempt to be faithful to the gospel. Essentially this has been achieved. Marginalized people have been made subjects in their relation to God and society. But being a church for the powerless does not necessarily mean being a church without power. The ILCO strives to be open and inclusive and at the same time maintain its strong public voice.

BRAZIL—IGREJA EVANGÉLICA DE CONFISSÃO LUTHERANA NO BRASIL, IECLB

Brazil is a huge country; roughly the same size as the whole of Europe.[70] When Spain and Portugal signed a treaty in 1494 that gave America to the

---

70. The text is mainly built on interviews and unprinted sources. The interviews are marked "interviews" in the footnotes and the informants' names are given in the

former and Africa and India to the latter, Brazil—not yet discovered by Europeans—was included in the "African" portion. The first European to visit Brazil was probably Cabral, in 1500.

Many of the native peoples were subsequently either killed by European invaders or died of diseases the latter brought with them. At first Brazil seemed to have little to attract Europeans. Things changed, however, and by the eighteenth century Brazil was a major supplier of both sugar and gold to the European market.

Brazil gained its independence in 1822, ruled by an emperor. The main export products at that time, coffee and rubber, were joined later on by sugar, cotton and cacao. Brazil became very prosperous but also very unequal socially. Many of the relatively few landowners had vast estates, while the rest of the rural population was largely landless. Various undemocratic regimes or military dictators ruled the country from the end of the nineteenth century up to the 1970s. Since the 1980s Brazil has been a democracy, though the political situation has remained rather complicated.

Today, Brazil is in many ways an economic superpower, but wealth is by no means distributed equally. Brazil's population numbers almost 200 million. There are huge assets in the form of forests, agricultural land and minerals. The main export items continue to be agricultural products such as sugar, coffee and tobacco but Brazil also has a huge industrial output. Despite the booming economy, unemployment is high, though on the decline; approximately 45 million people are believed to live in poverty, mostly in the interior and in the northeastern region. Brazil is often considered to be one of the most unequal countries in the world. Corruption is widespread and violence is another problem, with criminal gangs and police brutality. At the same time, compared to other Latin American countries, different ethnic groups live together in relative harmony in Brazil. The country also has a free school system, free health care and a pension system. All in all, Brazil is economically prosperous and normally considered to have a bright future; at the same time it has some major problems, such as deforestation and the vast differences between rich and poor, men and women, rural and urban inhabitants, indigenous people and others.

---

footnotes. The informants are listed in the bibliography under the heading "Interviews". The unprinted sources are marked "UP" in the footnotes and are listed in the bibliography under the heading "Unprinted sources".

The brief introductions to the countries are not footnoted; the information there is general knowledge, easily accessed in any guidebook.

To this profoundly Catholic country the first German immigrants arrived in 1824 with their Evangelical faith. Churches started to spread and there has been a Lutheran Synod since 1886. Its present official name, Igreja Evangélica de Confissão Luterana no Brasil (IECLB), dates from 1954.

Identity Foundations

Immigrants to Brazil from 1824 onwards came from a poor and starving northern Europe. The image of Brazil as a paradise which advertisements had taught them was very different from the reality many of them encountered. Making a living meant hard work on small farms or settling in remote areas to occupy the land and protect its borders from neighboring countries. The Brazilian government's main reason for allowing them to immigrate was the huge cost of keeping slaves plus the fear of a slave revolt such as had recently happened in Haiti and Bahia. Letting in Europeans was seen as a way to make Brazil more "white."[71] The remote locations of many of the new settlements—predominantly in the southern parts of Brazil—meant that there was hardly any contact between the new immigrants and the Portuguese-speaking population. Moreover, Brazilian law required that Protestant "worship should be private (i.e., could not take place in public), and had to be held in houses without any outward signs of a temple, which usually meant no towers or bells."[72] The Protestant immigrants were separated from the rest of the population in many ways and it was not until the end of the nineteenth century that they were granted full religious liberty.[73]

To survive in their new environment, the German immigrants generally formed their own communities, kept their native language, started their own schools, built places of worship and so on. Between 80 and 90 percent of them had a background in Lutheran churches but they called themselves "evangelical."[74]

As time went by, the small congregations created ecclesiastical structures, named synods. The first, Synod of Rio Grande do Sul, was established in 1886.[75] Later the synods developed relationships that eventually led to a Federation of Synods in 1949. They became members of the WCC in 1950 and the LWF in 1952. The Federation's name, Evangelical Church of the

71. Souza, Mauro. Interview.
72. Wachholz, "Lutheranism in Brazil," 2. UP.
73. Souza, Mauro. Interview.
74. Wachholz, "Lutheranism in Brazil," 3. UP.
75. Ibid.

Lutheran Confession in Brazil (IECLB), dates from 1954.[76] The Church and its congregations remained closely connected to Germany in many ways, at least until World War II. With the advent of Nazi Germany and Brazil's wartime position in relation to Germany, those communities faced hard times, partly because of the mistrust of anything German in Brazil.

> Breaking off diplomatic relations between Brazil and the *Reich* on August 22, 1942, due to pressure from the USA, led to greater excesses than during World War I: mass arrests of Germans, including pastors of the four synods, accused of belonging to the "fifth column", destruction of German property, for instance schools and temples, by people who had been instigated to do this . . .[77]

It was not until the end of World War II that the church gradually distanced itself from it's German identity. One step was the establishment of a Brazilian theological education—through the Escola Superior de Teologia—in São Leopoldo, Southern Brazil. Previously, all theological education had occurred in Germany.[78] Even today, however, the German roots are evident in the IECLB's identity, as are its roots in the rural areas. Or, as researcher Mauro Souza states, ". . . that is still the common view. The Lutheran Church is a German church and we are still figuring out what it means to be a church in the big cities."[79] Even so, the IECLB of to day is a huge church with very different kinds of work and it reaches far beyond the German descendants. It is a church with more than 700,000 members, 1,800 congregations, and 1,100 preaching points gathered in 489 parishes. There are 705 pastors, of whom 142 are women. There are almost 1,500 women's groups, 93 men's groups, and 715 youth groups. The IECLB has three radio stations and several periodicals; approximately 150 radio and TV programs are produced at congregational level.[80]

Brazil's Religious Setting

Brazilian society is highly religious. Pastor Douglas Wemuth expresses this by saying that every day a new church is created in Brazil.[81] He exaggerates

---

76. "Church Profile," 1. UP.
77. Wachholz, "Lutheranism in Brazil," 5.
78. Schmiedt Streck, Valburga. Interview.
79. Souza, Mauro. Interview.
80. "Church Profile," 2. UP.
81. Wemuth, Douglas. Interview.

but is right in saying that the religious landscape is changing—and changing fast. Roman Catholicism used to be Brazil's dominant religious tradition. Today, Brazil is becoming religiously pluralistic.[82] It is estimated that roughly two-thirds of the population are Catholic and the other third belong to one of the rapidly growing Pentecostal churches; moreover, there are probably twice as many Protestant pastors as Catholic priests. There are also the indigenous peoples' religions and Afro-Brasilian religions attract a relatively large number. Many Brazilians belong to more than one religion simultaneously. In addition, a significant number of people are leaving churches and traditional faith systems for a more secular life; it is thought that approximately 7 percent are secular.[83] These changes have, of course, predominantly affected the Catholic Church, which has lost many members in a relatively short period of time. But other churches, including the IECLB, are also affected in various ways.

Charismatic movements are having a considerable impact on Brazilian society today. This is not an entirely new phenomenon. The IECLB has experienced Charismatic renewals in the past. In the nineteenth century there were discussions between "converted" pastors who had studied at seminaries and "unconverted" who had studied at universities.[84] A pietistic mission started among Brazil's German population in 1927 and the Evangelical "Great Encounter Movement" began in the 1950s.[85] In the 1960s there were debates between the "sociopoliticals" and the "Evangelicals."[86] The effect of today's Pentecostal and Charismatic movements in Brazil is visible in the IECLB as a loss of some congregations, though probably not more than ten to fifteen.[87] However, it is important to stress that in some cases the parishioners were not aware of the fact that the congregation was leaving the IECLB; the decision in most cases was made by the pastor and the congregation's leaders.[88]

While the number of congregations that are actually leaving IECLB may be small, many more are being affected by the growth of the Neo-Pentecostal or Charismatic movements. There are at least two reasons for

82. Altmann, Walter. Interview.
83. Wemuth, Douglas. Interview.
84. Wachholz, "Lutheranism in Brazil," 19. UP.
85. Wemuth, Douglas. Interview.
86. Wachholz, "Lutheranism in Brazil," 19. UP.
87. Wemuth, Douglas. Interview.
88. Souza, Mauro. Interview.

this. One is that quite a few pastors in the IECLB are sympathetic to a more Evangelical type of theology and form of service. Probably about 20 percent of IECLB pastors consider themselves Evangelical but not in a way that would involve leaving the IECLB. They are Evangelical but within the Lutheran tradition. The other reason is that many congregations believe they have to change in various ways, whether they like it or not, in order not to lose members. Both groups are aware that the IECLB has to change, but for different reasons. One way in which this is happening is that some congregations try to make room for different forms of Evangelical theology or praxis, most often by providing alternative services, but they do so within their Lutheran tradition.[89] Douglas Wemuth describes his experiences:

> The majority of the congregations have a Lutheran service in the morning. Very liturgical, very traditional. That does not mean it is bad! But for some it is bad. . . . The majority have just the traditionalist service. But in the urban areas, especially in the big cities, you can find both kinds. I have worked for many years now in urban areas and I remember what it was like in my first congregation. A lot of Catholics were coming to our church—they were only Catholics by baptism—the majority said they didn't want the kind of service the Catholics had. They wanted something different. And this happened simultaneously in many places in Brazil. So we decided to have informal services. Many of those who came had a Catholic background. . . . And, also in my first congregation, a lot of young people from the university came. They, too, preferred informal services. First we had one on Sunday evenings, but not so often, then more often and now every Sunday evening at 9. Formal in the morning and informal in the evening.[90]

Most congregations have a traditional Lutheran service in the morning but quite a few, mostly in the cities, have started to have informal services in the afternoon or evening. In general, older people attend the morning service and younger people the informal service in the evening. But that is not always the case. Some people go to both and sometimes the older parishioners attend the informal service. All in all, the custom of having an informal evening service seems to be spreading.[91] From Wemuth's point of view, this in no way conflicts with the Lutheran tradition, even though he understands that some would say it does. The informal service is

89. Wemuth, Douglas. Interview.
90. Ibid.
91. Ibid.

Lutheran, he says, which can be seen in the sermon and in the fact that all the major parts of the traditional service are to be found in it. There is also a traditional view of the sacraments and in the absolute majority of parishes there are no special phenomena such as people speaking in tongues, which can be seen in many other churches and religious movements.[92]

The development of different forms of service is partly, as said, a consequence of the religious "market" being highly competitive. People are mobile and more ready than before to leave for something they think is better. The Lutheran church also needs to find new members and keep those it has got. Or, as the president of the IECLB, Walter Altmann, says:

> A few years ago we were not proselytizing Catholics. We put our strength into working with our own congregations. But at this point there is a great religious mobility. If we stay only inside we would constantly diminish, because there are always people who are leaving. But if we could be attractive to people who are looking around and who don't find anything that attracts them in other churches, that is good.[93]

An example of this is the creation of a new congregation in northern Brazil, in the city of São Luís. People there found the IECLB on the internet after searching for a more open and ecumenically positive church than what they were used to. The IECLB sent two ministers and the congregation is now part of the IECLB.[94] But while the IECLB needs to try to attract people who are looking for a church in which they feel at home, not ignoring other forms of religious manifestation, it is very important not to simply imitate successful movements and churches. "We should not plagiarize those who have momentary success and become popular at any price."[95] Being a Christian and being a church is something more and something other than what is often seen in these movements.[96]

A major challenge for the IECLB is of course how to maintain the inherited tradition in such a way that the IECLB remains a Lutheran church. Or as Wilhelm Wachholz writes, there is a constant tension in the IECLB which the church has to deal with.[97] How to be a church which respects

---

92. Ibid.
93. Altmann, Walter. Interview.
94. Ibid.
95. "God's Mission," 18. UP.
96. Ibid., 16–20.
97. Wachholz, "Lutheranism in Brazil," 19. UP.

religious plurality and simultaneously be a church with a clear Lutheran confession? The IECLB addressed this question in a document from 2000 on "religious pluralism":

> Simply expelling all those people who think and act differently cannot be the solution for situations of tension and conflict in the church. Doing that might mean that in the end there would be no one left. . . . The affirmation and strengthening of our unity, as well as the necessary fraternal discipline, cannot be based on the concept that some are saved and others are already lost. On the contrary, we should always remember the parable of the weeds mixed with the wheat (Matthew 13:24–30). The ultimate distinction between and separation of the two are not up to us and do not happen now. They are reserved for the Lord of the harvest when he returns. Also the Church's body bears the mark of all of us being sinners justified by faith and, as long as we live, at the same time righteous sinners. Consequently, we must always be attentive to the danger of falling into the temptation of taking on the role of the Pharisee who considered himself righteous, thanking God that he was not like the sinning publican (see Luke 18:9–14).[98]

The document opens up for different views and mentions "the other" with generosity. It sees a danger in a closed system, where right and wrong are simple categories. But while it does open up, it also emphasizes the importance of having an identity of one's own.

> However, in order to be able to preserve fraternal conviviality in the visible church (in this case, the IECLB itself), it is essential to have a basic consensus around the Lutheran doctrine, conduct and ethics. That is what has been suggested with the concept of a "minimum consensus", which respects legitimate diversity but preserves the conditions for church unity. . . . In other words, first of all we must positively affirm our confessional identity. This positive attitude is fundamental, and could be symbolized figuratively by the green traffic light, which allows us to move on.[99]

The task of being open and at the same time having a core identity is not easy. With a background in, and a living heritage from, the German immigrant group, although not so obvious as it used to be, for many years the IECLB has been trying to be a church with a wider scope than the German

---

98. *IECLB No Pluralisimo Religioso.* Cited in Wachholz, "Lutheranism in Brazil," 19. UP.

99. Ibid., 19.

ethnic church. In many ways it has succeeded. The IECLB could be described as a church in transition from German ethnicity to everyone, from the southern parts of Brazil to the whole country and from the countryside also to the large cities.

The Way to Be Church

One way in which the IECLB has tried to handle this transition has been to embrace different ways of being a Lutheran church, instead of splitting up into separate smaller and maybe more homogeneous churches. This has been done to a considerable extent with structural instruments. One important factor is the decentralization of power to the eighteen synods, which are now relatively autonomous.[100] Another is that the church recognizes three theological schools that differ in their theological approach, even though this might not be necessary since the number of graduates from these schools exceeds the number of ministers appointed by the church.[101] But the openness to pluralism is accompanied by an expectation from the church leadership that a minister is a minister for the whole church and should strive for the church's unity.[102]

One could say that the IECLB works along three major lines: what could be called Lutheran traditionalism, the Evangelical perspective and liberation theology. All three are to be found in the IECLB. Lutheran traditionalism, which has been the most important, is basically about maintaining the ways of administering the church and holding services (liturgy, language, music) that can be traced back to the era of immigration. This line is still very important but the IECLB is more than that. The Evangelical line, which is becoming even more important, stresses other aspects of theology and ecclesiastical practice, especially speaking of the power of the Holy Spirit, seeking to be more spontaneous and emphasizing personal emotional involvement. The line of liberation theology used to be evident in the work accomplished by Lutheran Popular Pastoral (PPL, Pastoral Popular Luterana), which attracted pastors and congregations whose approach to the church's role in society was more political. But as Walter Altmann says, even if liberation theology is important in the IECLB, in many ways it is searching for its form today. Being a voice for human rights is not

---

100. Souza, Mauro. Interview.
101. Ibid.
102. Ibid.

so straightforward with a civil government and democracy as it was under a military dictatorship.[103]

The IECLB endeavors to make room for different expressions of how to be a Lutheran within the church structure, and does this rather successfully. At the same time, the IECLB is acutely aware that the question of how to include different forms of Lutheran tradition is not the major problem so much as the fact that in many Lutheran families the tradition is becoming rather fragile. Religious tradition is no longer being handed down so clearly from parents to children. The IECLB expresses this in its Missionary Action Plan for the years 2008–12:

> Our greatest difficulties are in the transmission of tradition, especially in the urban context. Tradition is our spiritual, theological and ecclesiastical inheritance. The idea of transmitting the gospel from generation to generation is no longer automatic. Children do not necessarily follow their parents' religion anymore. The means of transmission of tradition weaken with the growth of individualism and religious pluralism.
>
> The increasing inability to reproduce our identity, especially in the urban context, is the central question to be understood and answered through the message and action of the church. The challenge is not only the loss of church members, but their permanence in the congregation with an identity connection. This can be a silent tragedy, perceivable, eventually, in the testimony of grandparents, when they speak of the difficulty of passing on their tradition. It is said, for example: "When I leave this life, my own descendants will not replace me. That place in the congregation will be empty."
>
> A growing number of people search for a religious experience that is unconnected with the message of a crucified God. New spiritualities look to worship the "I". These spiritualities are caught up in the here and now and do not consider the Christian hope of a new heaven and a new earth, coming from God. They are attracted to magical thinking, predominant in Brazil for centuries: manipulating spiritual forces for immediate and concrete benefits. The "I'll do you a favor, if you do me a favor" (toma lá, dá cá), so strongly present for centuries, is also a result of oppression and misery, which the majority endured for centuries. For this reason, the message and action of the Christian churches need to be articulated with a citizenship that strengthens itself, for example through social movements committed to an abundant life. God's

---

103. Altmann, Walter. Interview.

mission in the world occurs in different contexts. The IECLB is called to carry out its missionary task in the social, political, economic, cultural and religious Brazilian reality.[104]

The IECLB is seeking an answer by analyzing what its special contribution to Brazilian society today could be: "[w]e are challenged, as the IECLB, to use all of our capacities, gifts and resources for the common task of translating the richness of our spiritual inheritance to the next generations, in our Brazilian context."[105] One outcome of this is found in the structure of the Strategic Plan of Missionary Action. The four headings under which the IECLB aims to define its mission in accordance with God's mission and in relation to other churches are Education and Christian priesthood, Creative administration and resources, Mission and communication, and Creating new congregations.[106] The document spells out what the Lutheran tradition means when it comes to education. And the way in which it could be beneficial for people themselves, for the church and for society at large. This is followed by what Luther has to say about sustainability. Which aspects of its work does the church need to emphasize if it wants to be a sustainable church? How to do missionary work and communicate in a Lutheran church? What can we learn from our tradition about creating new and lasting congregations? The four topics are tied together by focusing on the Lutheran contribution and by trying to make use of every single person for the benefit of the church. No one is left out, everyone has a task in the IECLB's mission and in God's mission.[107] As a consequence of this Missionary Plan for the whole church, every congregation is now requested to create its own plan by applying the church plan to its own reality. In that way the IECLB hopes that the content of the national church plan can be a practical resource at the congregational level.[108]

Besides traditional congregational work, the IECLB has a huge and very diverse work in different areas. Matters of particular concern are (1) mission and growth, quantitatively and qualitatively, (2) confessional unity, (3) ecumenism, (4) dialogues with internal movements such as the Evangelicals and liberation theologians, (5) themes related to faith and money, grace and gratitude, (6) the church's public responsibility, (7) the relation

104. "God's Mission," 18–19. UP.
105. Ibid., 20.
106. Ibid., 55–77.
107. Ibid., 5–81.
108. "Church Profile," 3. UP.

between mission and diaconia with a holistic approach, (8) theological formation, (9) gender issues, and (10) issues of ethnical identities.[109] Each of these areas is dealt with by a special group in the church and they cover inner as well as outer aspects of being church. Identity questions are important today but so are socially related questions and have been for many years. For the IECLB it is important to be a prophetic voice in society, as Mauro Souza says. He goes on to say that the Lutheran church was active in the liberation theology movement from the very beginning in Brazil and had a distinctive voice. But he also considers that the church has to act differently today from what it did during the military regime. Walter Altmann also notes that being a critical public voice in a democracy is not as easy as it was with a military regime. He mentions land reforms and indigenous peoples and can see in both cases that the government is taking action but perhaps not enough. The church has to handle its criticism in a good way. He also says that there is sometimes a conflict between different rights. For instance, small farmers who were given land two generations ago often find it hard to understand how the church can go against them and advocate that the land be returned to the indigenous population. The IECLB puts a lot of effort into this work of mediating between different groups about land ownership.[110]

Despite these difficulties, the IECLB has a huge social work in practice, not least among landless people, children and poor people in urban areas.[111] The IECLB is also very active in analyzing, writing and speaking out about what it sees in society and how to relate that to the gospel. The social and economic situation in Brazil and its relation to the gospel is highly important for the IECLB.[112] On numerous occasions the IECLB has also spoken out against violations of human rights, not least discrimination against women, black people, indigenous and homosexuals, but also violence and protection of the environment.[113] In addition, questions external to Brazil have frequently been on the agenda. Walter Altmann mentions IECLB's role in protests against landmines and critique of the war in Iraq.[114] All in all, the IECLB has for a long time been a political and social voice

109. Ibid., 6.
110. Altmann, Walter. Interview.
111. "Church Profile," 6. UP.
112. Altmann, Walter. Interview.
113. Ibid.
114. Ibid.

in Brazil and has tried in different ways to form its members into political beings, based on Christ's commandments and active discipleship.[115]

The ecumenical commitment is another very important issue for the IECLB, which has been active for many years in various ecumenical bodies, both in Brazil and globally.

> The IECLB has in its constitution a clear commitment to the ecumenical vision. The church understands itself as having a link with the churches that confess Jesus Christ as Lord and Savior, in explicit accordance with the self-definition of the World Council of Churches. This ecumenical commitment is a major landmark in the identity of the IECLB and can be noticed today through a major participation and representation in decision-making processes and governing bodies of ecumenical organizations and endeavors nationally, continentally and globally.[116]

Women's Situation

Women have played and continue to play an important role in the IECLB. As in most societies and churches, it is mainly women who transfer the IECLB's religious tradition to children and grandchildren. They have kept the tradition alive. They have also been important "in the building of the IECLB—its temples, community halls, schools, hospitals, for example, as well as narrative and theology."[117] Even so, women have seldom been appreciated for what they do to the same degree as men. This is true in the IECLB as well as in most other churches.[118]

Women have been organized in the IECLB for a long time. The world's largest Lutheran organization for women is to be found there, Ordem Auxiliadora das Senhoras Evangélicas (OASE). The first group was founded in São Paulo in 1899 and now has more than 40,000 members. During its existence it has highlighted various working fields. At first it had more of an activist character; later the work was linked more closely to Bible reading, singing, and prayer.[119]

---

115. Ibid.
116. Schneider, "Role of Present-day 'Burning Issues,'" 3. UP.
117. Schmiedt Streck and Blasi, "Gender Issues and the Evangelical Church," 1. UP.
118. Blasi, Marcia. Interview.
119. Schmiedt Streck and Blasi, "Gender Issues and the Evangelical Church," 2–15. UP.

> Taking a closer look at the OASE today we can say that around 25 to 30 women gather in congregations to study the Bible, do handwork to be sold in bazaars and organize coffee parties also for gathering funds. According to the women "The Gospel is the foundation of the OASE and the love of Christ is its fuel." The OASE button (most women who belong to the group use the button) is an anchor cross on a blue ground: the blue is fidelity and the white represents the union of all colors and expresses joy, peace and purity. The women of the OASE confess: "That Jesus Christ is our hope, light, joy, peace, and justice. We want to be faithful and transmit this message to the world in words and in actions."[120]

Brazilian society is changing. Today, women go out to work and cannot be assumed to have time to take part in organizations like the OASE or even want to do so in the same way as they used to. Therefore the OASE is trying to find its form in this new society, trying to hold meetings in the evenings, introducing new subjects such as women's liberation and having open meetings for women outside the OASE. All in all, the OASE is undergoing a transformation.[121] Closely intertwined with the OASE, the IECLB has the Evangelical Lutheran Sisterhood. The first sisters arrived from Germany in 1909 and the work ever since has been in schools and kindergartens, the elderly and nursing.[122]

The first woman to undertake theological training did so in 1966 and the IECLB's first woman pastor was ordained in 1982. Today there are 142 women pastors, twenty-seven sisters, fifty-six catechists, sixty-four deaconesses, and nine missionaries. But although women have access to ministry and emphasize different matters, besides playing an important role in other respects in the IECLB, problems still exist. Brazilian society is in many ways patriarchal, which affects women in general and in their role as pastors, though the problems are less evident than they used to be.

> Women in ministry aknowledge that ordination does not give them a special power, but a power to share in accordance with the Gospel. In this respect, women pastors have contributed reflections on the work of women in the church. Issues such as domestic violence, patriarchy, human rights also for women, have become part of the Church's agenda in great part because of women's voice and witness. The presence and the work of women in ministry

---

120. Ibid., 4.
121. Ibid.
122. Ibid., 4–5.

have also helped to open the way for women to be elected as church leaders...[123]

In general, a major problem for women in ministry is the feeling of guilt. Guilt for provoking ruptures with tradition. Guilt from feeling that we are not doing enough. Guilt for not being adequate, which is probably the most dangerous form of guilt. If women are not aware of gender imbalances, they tend to take being rejected personally. My experience as a parish minister has shown me that I am criticized not because I am Marcia but because I am a woman. It would be the same with any other woman minister. The greatest challenge for us is to bear sorrow and pain alongside hopes and dreams, and to keep walking.[124]

This picture is shared by others. Mauro Souza says that the popular culture is very sexist and that this affects the whole of society, including the church. For instance, he says that a woman has to work twice as hard as a man to be accepted and that not many congregations want a woman pastor. That partly reflects their attitude to women pastors and is partly due to the fact that with a male pastor, the congregation will probably also get a pastor's wife working in the parish. With a female pastor, the husband is unlikely to do that kind of work. But even if there are problems, he says that the IECLB has done a lot when it comes to gender. People outside the church also acknowledge that, not least the work against domestic violence, says Mauro Souza.[125] Walter Altmann says that a lot still remains to be done both in society in general and in the church when it comes to gender, but the situation within the church is not bad; 25 percent of the pastors are women, he says, and there is a special gender desk in the church. However, according to him, there are too few women in top positions in the church; for instance, there is only one female synodal pastor.[126]

Theology

The IECLB is a church with a background in German education and German theology. It is a theologically reflective church in theory and in practice, as can be seen in published documents on various subjects. It is also a church working with what its Lutheran heritage means today and with how

123. Ibid., 8.
124. Blasi, Marcia. Interview.
125. Souza, Mauro. Interview.
126. Altmann, Walter. Interview.

to be a church in Brazilian society. Mauro Souza says that for some it is being a Christian that is most important and being a Lutheran comes second, while others say it should be the other way round.[127] Walter Altmann sees Luther as more important than Lutheranism, but not even Luther should be taken uncritically. He goes on to say that for the IECLB it is most important to find its own questions, from its own reality, and then go to Luther. Instead of letting Luther answer the questions, they should meet and see what the outcome will be. He believes that what is most important for the IECLB today is to refrain from separating the religious and worldly realms. They cannot be separated. He also points to the dignity of the human being, and justification by grace. "God has given every single person an infinite value, without any merit. So if people are deprived of basic human rights, we as church in consequence have to strive for every human being's rights."[128] Mauro Souza also reflects along these lines when he says that he is Lutheran and gets everything by grace from God, but in return he has to do things for others.[129] Briefly, what Altmann and Souza are saying is expressed in the Missionary Action plan, under the heading "Theology and Missionary Vision: God's Passion for the World."

> God did not make us in his image and likeness by chance. In doing this, he invites us, as man and woman, to live with one another in that which was given to us in creation which is most beautiful and marvelous: love. It is God's love that gives life to the universe, which invites us to solidarity, fraternity, sharing and communion with one another. It is this love which calls us to restoration and brings us to contemplate and take care of God's creation with passion and love. It is God's love that makes us see, with him, that everything that he made is good.[130]

> It is in Christ Jesus that God shows his greatest and most beautiful act of love to all people. It is in Christ that the signs of God's kingdom have already become real in our midst: the sick are healed; children are valued; women are defended against accusing men; laws that harm the love for your neighbor are questioned; sinners and people of bad reputation are heard, valued and transformed;

---

127. Souza, Mauro. Interview.
128. Altmann, Walter. Interview.
129. Souza, Mauro. Interview.
130. "God's Mission," 30. UP.

strangers are blessed, the dead are resurrected; true servanthood is taught.[131]

Our response to God's love revealed in Jesus Christ, however, is: "Crucify him!" Jesus, nevertheless, intercedes for us: "Father, forgive them! For they do not know what they are doing." However, it is on the cross that God reveals his love and greatest passion for the world.[132]

Out of love for humanity, God resurrects Jesus Christ and answers his son's request: "I will ask the Father, and He will give you another Counselor, the Spirit of truth, to be with you forever." It is under the power of the Holy Spirit that all the Christian community— scattered, depressed and frightened by the death of Jesus Christ— is reanimated for life: "However, when the Holy Spirit comes upon you, you will receive power and you will be my witnesses in Jerusalem, and in all Judea and Samaria, and to the ends of the earth." It is under the power of the Holy Spirit that the apostles are encouraged to witness to that which they saw and heard of God's passion revealed in our Lord and Savior Jesus Christ. It is under the power of the Holy Spirit that men and women, as Christian history proceeds, do not allow themselves to be intimidated by people and civil and religious authorities that usurped and used the gospel for their own interests. It is under the power of the Holy Spirit that our gifts are manifested and put to work for life.[133]

To conclude, theology in the IECLB is moving in different directions depending on the context in which it is done. There is liberation theology, there is more Evangelical theology and there is "traditional" Lutheranism and others. But the church sticks together because of its permissive attitude and the conviction that to be a church is to be a church for others.

Summary

Because of its history, the IECLB has directed its work at the German ethnic group in Brazil. It has willed this and external circumstances have also played a part. The external pressure has decreased but the ethnic orientation has not changed to the same extent. Even so, the IECLB has had

---

131. Ibid., 31.
132. Ibid., 30.
133. Ibid., 32.

a strong voice—within its capacity as a relatively small church that is not tightly knit to the State—during the years of dictatorship and in other issues concerning human value and dignity. With today's changing society, the preconditions for the IECLB have changed rapidly and the church must now find a way out of its former boundaries without losing important parts of its identity.

Historically, the IECLB has been an alternative to the major culture in Brazil but not with the purpose of giving people in Brazil an alternative. It has been more of a closed alternative, apparently open to everyone but not actually looking for members outside the ethnic group of Germans descendants. Today, the trend seems to be that the IECLB is opening up to the rest of society. This is partly because that is essential if it does not want to lose members, and partly because the need for a German church in Brazil is not what it was some years ago. Essentially, the new generations of German descendants in Brazil see themselves as Brazilians rather than Germans.

Today, with a rapidly changing religious landscape, what the IECLB has done in the past cannot be repeated in the same way. The IECLB is trying to solve this by, for example, opening up for new ways of holding church services. But besides trying to find new ways to attract young people and new people, it tries to preserve the old forms so as not to lose the old identity. That means that the church's identity is changing. In an attempt to open up, the IECLB also tries to work with different church traditions simultaneously: the older Germans, the Evangelicals and liberation theology. The task for the future is to change what needs to be changed without losing the core identity. For a long time the IECLB was a church for rather poor people in remote areas of the country. That is now changing; this group of members no longer exists, at least not generally. The former German immigrants now belong to the middle class and other groups make up the poor.

ICELAND—ÞJÓÐKIRKJAN, ELCI

Iceland is a small country with only 320,000 inhabitants, of whom two-thirds live in the Reykjavík area on the southwest coast.[134] Iceland is the

134. The text is mainly built on interviews and unprinted sources. The interviews are marked "interviews" in the footnotes and the informants' names are given in the footnotes. The informants are listed in the bibliography under the heading "Interviews". The unprinted sources are marked "UP" in the footnotes and are listed in the bibliography under the heading "Unprinted sources".

The brief introductions to the countries are not footnoted; the information there is general knowledge, easily accessed in any guidebook.

least densely populated country in Europe; only one-fifth of its area is populated at all and much less is cultivated. There are active volcanoes and much of the landscape is characterized by lava in the form of stones or sand. There are also geysers and huge glaciers, among them Vattnajökull, the third largest glacier in the world.

The island was first populated more permanently by Norwegian Vikings in the ninth century. A union of Iceland and Norway lasted from 1286 to 1536, when Iceland became a vassal state of Denmark. Iceland finally became an independent state in union with Denmark in 1918 and the Republic of Iceland was founded in 1944.

Iceland has been prosperous in many ways. A main source of income is the fishing industry; Iceland's territorial waters are seven times larger than the country itself, a fact that has led to conflicts with other nations. There are also rich sources of hydro power, and hot springs are used for central heating all over the country. The huge—and therefore cheap—supply of hydro power has also aided the development of an efficient aluminum industry which now seems likely to outdo the fishing industry. Another industry that is expanding rapidly is tourism, with almost 600,000 visitors a year. When an economic decline hit Europe in the late 1980s, Iceland's active management achieved a return to growth from 1995 onwards. All went well until the banking system collapsed in 2008, leading to huge protests throughout the country. The economy is still affected, though many of the early dire predictions about the country's future have not materialized. Unemployment has been reduced to 5.8 percent, still a high figure for Iceland but low compared to the rest of Europe. The banking system is functioning again and growth is picking up.

Iceland's population is notably homogeneous, mostly made up of Norwegian descendants and other Nordic immigrants, though settlers today are also coming from other countries. Life expectancy is the second highest in the world: 82 years for women, 79 for men. There is universal free healthcare and a well-developed educational system. School is compulsory from six to sixteen years of age and 93 percent go on to higher education. There are several universities despite the small population. There are a number of newspapers and the largest is free and funded by advertisements. There are both state and privately owned radio and TV channels. The parliament, founded in the year 930, is the oldest in the world; the ninety-three members, as well as Iceland's president, are elected every fourth year.

There is an active cultural life. The capital, Reykjavík, has an opera house, a symphony orchestra and a national theatre. Iceland also has a long history of writers and books. Many of the classical works date from the twelfth and thirteenth centuries and some texts are from the tenth century. Also in modern times Iceland has produced a variety of cultural personalities in literature, music and film. Iceland ranks first in the world in the number of books published per capita.

Christianity was established as the religion of Iceland in the year 1000 but belief in the ancient Norse gods was never opposed very actively. Iceland has been Evangelical Lutheran since the mid-sixteenth century. Today, just over 76 percent of the population belong to the Evangelical Lutheran Church of Iceland (ELCI) but—as in all Nordic folk churches—the number who take an active part in church matters and services is much smaller. About 10 percent of the population attend a church service once a month.

A National or a Folk Church

Icelanders have a history of being a spiritual people living close to nature. They believe in God and pray but preferably keep their religion to themselves.[135] Or as pastor Auður Eir Vilhjálmsdóttir, says: "they are not 'churchgoers.'"[136] An illustration of this is that spiritism has played and still plays an important role for many Icelanders; it even used to be found inside the church but that is no longer the case.[137] Pastor Árni Svanur Danielsson says that Icelanders are in favor of spirituality but not dogma. The ELCI has therefore developed into a church that deals more with Christian life than with church dogma.[138] He also says that another reason for this could be the country's isolated location: "There was no one with whom we could compare ourselves and no one asked about us." All in all, various circumstances have made the ELCI what it is today, a huge church that covers the whole country, considered by most people to be *the* church, but at the same time a church which struggles with what that means in present-day Iceland.[139] The ELCI is by law the national church and also Iceland's folk church; as such it is deeply intertwined with Icelandic history, culture, civil society, and politics.

135. Björnsdóttir, Steinunn Arnþrúður. Interview.
136. Vilhjálmsdóttir, Auður Eir. Interview.
137. Björnsdóttir, Steinunn Arnþrúður. Interview.
138. Danielsson, Árni Svanur. Interview.
139. Ibid.

In 1998, just over a year before the celebration of Iceland's millennium as a Christian country, the ELCI produced a brochure stressing its identity, not as Evangelical Lutheran but rather as national Icelandic, writes researcher Hjalti Hugason.[140] He adds that the brochure noted a continuity from the early Catholic Church over the Reformation to the church of today. That continuity consists in the fact that the church in Iceland is both the country's national church and a church for everyone. The transition from a Catholic to a Lutheran church was influenced by practical and political circumstances; and while it is labeled differently, the ELCI has never ceased to be a church for the Icelandic people.[141] Others seem to confirm that opinion. According to pastor Sigurður Árni Þórðarson, the ELCI of today is defined much more by Icelandic culture and history than by a Lutheran heritage,[142] while pastor Steinunn Arnþrúður Björnsdóttir says that the Icelandic people are Christian but cannot be said to be more explicitly Lutheran. The ELCI is a Lutheran church but is seen by many as first and foremost a folk church. But what being a folk church means is less clear and opinions differ.[143]

As in the other Nordic countries, the ties between church and state have been close in Iceland ever since the sixteenth century, when the church in Iceland became Lutheran. As a vassal of Denmark, in 1665 Iceland became a part of a confessional state established on an Evangelical Lutheran ground. In 1874, during debates about independence, Iceland got a new constitution in which §45 states that "The Evangelical Lutheran church is the Icelandic folk church and is supported and protected by the public sector."[144] Later, the public sector became the state. Today, Icelandic society is changing rapidly in many ways. People are leaving the countryside for an urban life, immigrants are arriving and secularization is spreading. More people than before are leaving the ELCI; there are other religions and denominations.[145] All this has led the ELCI and the Icelandic state to work on what it means that the ELCI is *one* church in Iceland, not *the* church. One result is that today the ELCI is regulated by legislation on the folk church (no. 78/1997), which implies that the ELCI is essentially a free church when

---

140. Hugason, "Kyrka-stat relationen i Island," 3. UP.
141. Ibid., 3.
142. Þórðarson, Sigurður Árni. Interview.
143. Björnsdóttir, Steinunn Arnþrúður. Interview.
144. Hugason, "Kyrka-stat relationen i Island," 4. UP.
145. Danielsson, Árni Svanur. Interview.

it comes to its work, organization, teaching and so on. At the same time, the ELCI has a special status, not least in economic matters.[146] Moreover, the ELCI has much more access to the public arena than other denominations and religions. The opening of parliament begins with a service in the cathedral; the public radio broadcasts services from the ELCI; schools cooperate with the ELCI and so on.[147] The reasons for this special status are historical and go back many centuries. But events in the past century have also been important for the construction of the ELCI's identity and therefore for its relationship with the state. One example is the deepening of this relationship as a consequence of the ELCI's role in the creation of the Icelandic state in connection with the separation from Denmark in 1944.[148] At the same time, as the folk church of Iceland, the ELCI is a church with historical bonds to the whole of society, a church that has the whole of Iceland as its field and a church that is open to everyone.[149]

The Church and Iceland Today

The ELCI is the main religious body in Iceland, with work in every part of the country. There are about 280 parishes, served by approximately 150 pastors and thirty deacons. There is one bishop, located in Reykjavík, and two suffragan bishops, in Skalholt and Holar.[150] Most of the ELCI's work is done by or in parishes. In addition to a church building, many parishes have other facilities for various activities: meeting places, playgrounds for children and so on.[151] Sunday worship does not normally attract a lot of people but weekday activities are popular and most people also use the church for baptisms, weddings and funerals. Seven out of ten children are baptized in their first year, a large proportion of adolescents are confirmed, 80 percent are married in church and the absolute majority of funerals take place in church.[152] The relation between church and people is very close, especially in the countryside, but it has proved to be harder to maintain as rural people move to Reykjavík.[153] Besides the work done by the parishes,

146. Hugason, "Kyrka-stat relationen i Island," 9–11. UP.
147. Ibid., 14.
148. Ibid., 22–23.
149. "Policy document ELCI, 2003." UP.
150. Björnsdóttir, Sigurður Árni. Interview.
151. Ibid.
152. Hugason, Hjalti. Interview.
153. Danielsson, Árni Svanur. Interview.

the ELCI is engaged in many fields at the national level, such as an organization for church aid, a family counseling center, a music school, a publishing house, a forum for interfaith dialogue, and so on. The diverse activities cover socially related fields as well as more theological matters. That is also how the ELCI would like to be seen. A policy document from 2003 states that the ELCI's vision is for the folk church to be a vital and powerful movement of people who journey together in faith in God through Jesus Christ. It is a visible, colorful, and growing communion that awakens and nourishes Christian worship and spirituality. The church meets everyone on his/her journey, and provides service and shelter. The ELCI is a forum for social dialogue in the light of the Christian faith, and it empowers people to serve God and neighbor.[154]

But while through history the church has lived in a close relationship with the people and met them on their journey through life—as the vision says—according to pastor Gunnar Kristjánsson there are those who mean that in the second half of the twentieth century the ELCI has become more conservative and thereby lost some of the confidence it had among Icelandic people. A shift in the church's direction is said to be one reason; another is that for a long time the teachers in the small faculty at the university where the pastors mostly are educated were rather conservative.[155] Today, however, very few ELCI pastors can be said to be very conservative, maybe 5 to 7 percent, but they are vocal, according to Sigurður Árni Þórðarson. This has been evident, for example, in issues such as same-sex marriage[156] and women's rights.[157] He goes on to say that nowadays the person in the street sees the church as old-fashioned.[158] His conclusion is that the way forward should be to engage in ecological questions, gender discussion and questions about value, but that is not yet the case.[159] The church service is generally considered rather boring. But while the number who question the church or its teaching is rising, Icelanders are still a praying people; 92 percent are said to have been taught to pray at home.[160] Moreover, Steinunn

---

154. "Policy document ELCI, 2003," 2–3. UP.
155. Kristjánsson, Gunnar. Interview.
156. Bóasdóttir, "Den kyrkliga debatten." UP.
157. Þórðarson, Sigurður Árni. Interview.
158. Ibid.
159. Ibid.
160. Björnsdóttir, "How Lutheran?" UP.

Arnþrúður Björnsdóttir, says that people who are reasonably active in church work are more numerous than ever before.[161]

At the same time, there is something new in the relationship between people and the church. An important factor here is the severe economic crisis that hit Iceland some years ago, a crisis that affected the whole of society and every individual. Officials and other members of the church took leading roles in trying to deal with the consequences. Many pastors were very explicit; churches were opened up for people in need and efforts were made to provide emergency assistance. Members of the ELCI, pastors and others, worked along two lines, first by helping people in immediate trouble and second by trying to find solutions on a more structural level.[162] This active involvement during the economic crisis, with the church's critical public voice, has brought people into contact with the church in a new way. But it has also faced the church with questions of identity. What is the ELCI today and what is its role in Icelandic society?[163]

Being a Lutheran Church

The ELCI is a Lutheran church and has been so for the last 500 years. It is a member of the LWF and Icelandic law requires it to be Lutheran. At the same time, a common opinion seems to be that neither Luther nor Lutheran theology plays a very important role in what is happening in the ELCI.[164] Steinunn Arnþrúður Björnsdóttir illustrates this with a story:

> A young Icelander newly arrived at a large US university some 30 years ago applied for a room to share in a dormitory. The first question he got from a prospective roommate was: What church do you belong to? The surprised Icelander remembered vaguely that the Church of Iceland was called Evangelical Lutheran. So he explained that his religion was "Evangelical Lutheran." The prospective roommate hung up.[165]

She explains that the description "Evangelical Lutheran" meant nothing to the other student. He knew that "Lutheran" referred in some way to Martin Luther but was not clear what that meant. Neither is "Evangelical"

---

161. Björnsdóttir, Steinunn Arnþrúður. Interview.
162. Danielsson, Árni Svanur. Interview.
163. Ibid.
164. Ibid.
165. Björnsdóttir, Steinunn Arnþrúður. Interview.

commonly used in Iceland to define the church.¹⁶⁶ While it is true that "Lutheran" and "Evangelical" are used to define or describe the ELCI, what these words stand for is not common knowledge.¹⁶⁷ Instead, the ELCI is described much more frequently as "the Icelandic folk church." Steinunn Arnþrúður Björnsdóttir accordingly asks whether it is possible to see the seven marks of the Church which Martin Luther used to define a true church as applicable to the way in which the ELCI is structured and manages its work. She concludes:

> Is the ELCI a Lutheran church? Would a "poor confused person" be able to recognize it as a Christian assembly? The Marks of the Church as put forward by Martin Luther in "On the councils and the Churches" are all visible to some extent in the ELCI, as seen by the members of the church, lay and ordained. Surveys only tell a part of the story but they do give us insight into what people think and how they feel about the ELCI and some aspects of its work, such as pastors and the liturgy. It is clear from these surveys that expectations of pastors are great, and Martin Luther's admonition, "you should put up with him", does not match people's ideas about the pastor. First and foremost the pastor needs to be good at counselling, but also a good preacher, liberal and good with people. The results reflect different times, perhaps different needs and in some respect greater expectations and less tolerance of representatives of the pastoral profession than in the 16th century. On the other hand, they reflect much more liberal views about the church's religious teaching than in Luther's day.¹⁶⁸

The ELCI must be understood as a Lutheran church—but a Lutheran church in transition, Steinunn Arnþrúður Björnsdóttir says. The ELCI has been the church for the Icelandic people for a very long time and in being that it has leaned on its Lutheran tradition. But it is not just the Lutheran tradition which has defined or shaped the ELCI through history. Earlier, in a relatively homogeneous society, it was easier to see the ELCI as a Lutheran church, because there was nothing else to compare with, she says.¹⁶⁹

---

166. Ibid.
167. Ibid.
168. Björnsdóttir, "How Lutheran?," 28. UP.
169. Björnsdóttir, Steinunn Arnþrúður. Interview.

Structure and Leadership

Each parish in the ELCI is a financially independent unit. Together with the pastor, it is responsible for the upkeep of the church building and for everything that is being done in the parish, such as youth work, teaching, pastoral care and other things. The state pays the pastor's salary but that is to be understood as compensation for the church estates that were transferred to the state during the twentieth century.[170] Over the parishes are nine deaneries. There is also a bishop's office, a church Council and a General Synod.

> The General Synod is the supreme authority in the affairs of the Evangelical Lutheran Church of Iceland. The General Synod is composed of 29 elected representatives: 12 members of the clergy and 17 lay members. The bishop of Iceland, the two suffragan bishops and one representative from the University of Iceland's theological faculty are non-voting members, with the right to speak and propose motions. The General Synod elects a president from among the lay delegates. The General Synod passes regulations for the church, forms strategies for various fields of operations and reviews financial affairs under the command of the Church Council. The General Synod may initiate bills concerning church matters and it may request that the Minister of Ecclesiastical Affairs propose such a bill in the Alltingi. The minister must request the opinion and recommendations of the General Synod regarding bills that deal with church matters.
>
> The Church Council is the Executive branch of the Evangelical Lutheran Church of Iceland. It executes decisions regarding the common affairs of the church, including tasks delegated by law to the Church Council as well as matters referred to the council by the General Synod, the Pastoral Synod, the Lay People's Council, the Altingi and the Government to the extent that such matters have not been entrusted to the Bishop of Iceland or to other church institutions. The Church Council is elected by the General Synod and is under its direction. The Bishop of Iceland is ex officio president of the Church Council.
>
> The Office of the Bishop of Iceland is where the administrative facilities of the Bishop of Iceland as well as the administration of the church Council and the General Synod are located. The Bishop's office has multiple functions relating to the administration and bookkeeping of the church and provides various services for the funds and institutions of the church; it represents the Evangelical

---

170. Hugason, "Kyrka-stat relationen i Island," 14–15. UP.

Lutheran Church of Iceland with regard to the Church's common interests, its relationships and collaboration with various institutions as well as its foreign relations.[171]

All in all, the ELCI has a democratic structure. But in that structure the bishop has an important role and some say it is becoming even stronger at the expense of the General Synod.[172] One of the most important matters for the bishop is to try to reconcile or combine different positions in the church.[173]

A recent example of how a decision can be made in the ELCI is the debate about same-sex marriage. Briefly, the debate lasted for some 15 years, in Icelandic society as well as in the ELCI, with each influencing the other. Both church and state tried to get the other party to make decisions which they themselves did not favor. As Sólveig Anna Bóasdóttir shows, the question was discussed back and forth, with the state and society constantly taking the lead.[174] At times the church said it could not advocate same-sex marriage because there was no basis for that in law; the state in turn said it wanted to have the ELCI on its side before making that decision.[175] After many years of debate, a newly elected government said that it was in favor of giving religious organizations the right to perform civil partnership registrations. After a heated debate, the General Synod decided that if parliament decided to allow religious organizations to perform civil partnership registrations, pastors in the ELCI should be allowed to do this. Parliament took that decision a few months later. In a survey, 77 percent of the pastors were positive, 7 percent said they would not do it. The bishop did not answer.[176] Some people say that while his office gives the bishop a good deal of power, he failed to find a good balance in this discussion; it was rather the case that his actions and what he said aggravated the conflict.[177] The church was in need of leaders who can unite different perspectives and keep together, as Sigurður Árni Þórðarson says.[178] When a single act of marriage

---

171. "The Church of Iceland." 3. UP.
172. Kristjánsson, Gunnar. Interview.
173. Þórðarson, Sigurður Árni. Interview.
174. Bóasdóttir, "Den kyrkliga debatten." UP.
175. Bóasdóttir, Sólveig Anna. Interview.
176. Bóasdóttir, "Den kyrkliga debatten," 7. UP.
177. Þórðarson, Sigurður Árni. Interview.
178. Ibid.

was finally decided in 2010, an organization for gays and lesbians awarded a prize to 111 persons in the church for their help in accomplishing this.[179]

Women's Situation

Icelandic society can be said to be open and liberal, with the ability to absorb progressive ideas.[180] It is also relatively equal. Women were granted equal access to public offices in 1911 and have had the right to vote since 1915. In 1980 Vigdís Finnbogadóttir became the world's first female president and in 2009 Jóhanna Sigurðardóttir became probably the world's first openly lesbian head of government. There is also a women's party in parliament, to some extent forcing the other parties to be more engaged in women's issues.[181] But of course there are also inequalities in Iceland. Wages, for example, are still lower for women than for men.

Women in Iceland have had the right to study theology for ordained ministry since 1886 but it was not until 1974 that the ELCI's first female pastor was ordained, followed by the second in 1981. Today, almost a third of all pastors in the ELCI are women. The then bishop took the decision to ordain women after discussions with the pastors' association and the Church Council. He said that he could not see any theological obstacles to ordination, neither did he believe that it would lead to a major schism in the church.[182] Today, two of the three bishops are women; the first was ordained in June 2012 and the second later that year.[183] Since 1999 the ELCI has had a policy plan on gender issues to promote the status of women in the church. The background is the Icelandic law on equal rights of men and women, as well as the positions in church organizations such as the LWF and the WCC. The five-point gender equality plan is the ELCI's response to this and demonstrates the ELCI's interest in creating this equality.[184]

> to improve the status of women within the church
> to enforce gender equality within committees and church administrations
> to promote equal pay and rights
> to provide training and teaching material regarding gender issues
> to reconsider language used within the church.[185]

179. Danielsson, Árni Svanur. Interview.
180. Bóasdóttir, "Den kyrkliga debatten," 1. UP.
181. Bóasdóttir, Sólveig Anna. Interview.
182. Guðmundsdóttir, Arnfríður. Interview.
183. Danielsson, Árni Svanur. Interview.
184. Guðmundsdóttir, Arnfríður. Interview.
185. Gender Equality Plan.

Since then the ELCI has worked on implementing the plan and has stated that everyone working in the church is obliged to follow it.[186] Moreover, a new translation of the Bible started in 2007 with the intention that large parts will use an inclusive language. The remaining passages will be those that are used in the church liturgy.[187] But while much is being done in the ELCI to foster equality, there is still some way to go. Men are still over-represented in the church leadership—vicars and chairpersons in parish assemblies—especially in the Reykjavík area.[188]

A notable feature of the ELCI is the Women's Church, an independent internal group founded in 1993. The work there has to do, not least, with feminist theology. It involves using inclusive language and talk about God in a feminine gender. Regular meetings are held in different churches to discuss various topics and a service is celebrated once a month using a new liturgy. According to Auður Eir Vilhjálmsdóttir, the Women's Church has had a large impact on the ELCI and what is done there is a part of a Lutheran heritage.[189] They are giving the Bible back to people and also making way for people to decide for themselves in matters of faith, and that is Lutheran. Both men and women take part in the activities of the Women's Church and those who are active are committed to the Christian belief and to questions of gender. To be a member of the Women's Church is a bigger step than it is to be a member of the folk church.[190]

Summary

The ELCI is a national church with a focus on openness. It could also be said that the ELCI is a church that lives in many ways in symbioses with the state and Icelandic culture. For various reasons these relationships are now beginning to be discussed more seriously than before. This was evident, for example, during the protests in connection with the economic crises, when the church had a public voice.

The ELCI lives in the tension between tradition and renewal. Many things are still done as they have been done for a long time, other things are changing. For example, the service is—essentially—still done in a

---

186. Guðmundsdóttir, Arnfríður. Interview.
187. Ibid.
188. Ibid.
189. Vilhjálmsdóttir, Auður Eir. Interview.
190. Ibid.

traditional way, while moral and ethical views normally follow the general view in society, with a slight delay.

The priests were normally seen as ordinary people in the village. This is still the case in many respects, but the church also has access to the state in a very special way. It has most of the population as members, a good reputation and people's confidence and is accordingly a powerful institution with the ability to influence people and society in a profound way.

MADAGASCAR—FIANGONANA LOTERANA MALAGASY, FLM

Madagascar is one of the world's largest islands.[191] The capital Antananarivo, situated on a plateau in the center of the country, has roughly 1.4 million inhabitants and the country itself 20 million. Because of the island's early split from the rest of the continent, its nature and wildlife have developed independently in many ways. Many species do not occur elsewhere, a fact for which Madagascar is renowned. Madagascar's culture is rather special, due to the island having been populated from two directions, Asia and Africa. The Asian population arrived from Indonesia around two thousand years ago. Today the population is mixed but is generally more Asian in the inland and more African on the coast.

Arabic traders began to settle on the island in the sixteenth century and Europeans occasionally visited after the island's "discovery" in 1500. But almost three centuries passed before Europeans ventured into the inland. At the same time, the late eighteenth century, the process of unifying the various tribes on the island was started by King Andrianampoinimerina of the Merina tribe, who also moved the capital to today's Antananarivo. During the reign of Queen Ranavalona I (1828–61) relations with Europe were bad and Christianity was forbidden. Relations between, mostly, Great Britain, France, and Madagascar then became closer and the island was a French colony from 1896. An uprising in 1947 was brutally crushed by French troops, with 80,000 people killed, and Madagascar eventually became independent in 1960. Since then, Madagascar has experienced many political

---

191. The text is mainly built on interviews and unprinted sources. The interviews are marked "interviews" in the footnotes and the informants' names are given in the footnotes. The informants are listed in the bibliography under the heading "Interviews". The unprinted sources are marked "UP" in the footnotes and are listed in the bibliography under the heading "Unprinted sources".

The brief introductions to the countries are not footnoted; the information there is general knowledge, easily accessed in any guidebook.

shifts. It functioned as a socialist state from 1975 to 1990—albeit with more than one approved party—leaning on China, North Korea, and the Soviet Union. But lack of food, corruption and unemployment frequently led to unrest and finally to a more open, but very unstable, political situation. Unrest still characterizes the country. Andry Rajoelina commanded a military coup in 2009, which led to Madagascar's exclusion from the African Union (AU). Since then the political situation has been chaotic, with allegations from all sides.

Madagascar is a poor country despite all its natural resources, not least minerals. Oil deposits were found along the coast in the 1980s but are still largely unexploited. There have been attempts to develop a tourist industry. The poverty has several explanations. One is that the political and economic situation has been unstable for many years. Another is the lack of electricity and an undeveloped transportation system. Unemployment is rife; six out of ten people in Antananarivo are believed to have an informal income. There is compulsory education for everyone up to the age of thirteen but many have to quit school before that; only 7 percent of fifteen- to eighteen-year-olds attend school. There is constant tension between the cities and the even poorer countryside, where roads are bad or unusable in some seasons and electricity is almost nonexistent. About 80 percent of the population are located in rural areas and make a living out of farming but agricultural land makes up only 10 percent of the island. A lot more is used for cattle, which is a more traditional occupation. About 70 percent of the population is believed to live in poverty.

Today, 50 percent of the population is believed to belong to various Christian denominations, 7 percent are Muslim and the rest belong to traditional religions. Many mix Christianity with traditional beliefs. In this country we find Fiangonana Loterana Malagasy (FLM), the fast-growing Lutheran church in Madagascar.

The Identity Base

With three million members, the FLM is the world's ninth largest Lutheran church. And it is growing fast. Norwegian missionaries started their work in Madagascar in 1866 and the American Lutheran Church followed just over twenty years later, in 1888. These two mission churches merged in 1950 to form a single autonomous church, the FLM. Today the church covers the whole country with 5000 congregations and 1,200 ministers.

The FLM is Madagascar's third largest Christian denomination. It has good ecumenical relations with Catholics, Anglicans and the Reformed church, but also a clear identity of its own. Joseph Randrianasolo comments that the FLM is not just a Protestant church, it is a Lutheran church. He writes that "[t]he Malagasy Lutheran Church [FLM] believes and accepts that the Holy Scriptures, that is, the canonical books in the Old Testament and the New Testament, are the word of God. It is the Holy Scriptures that constitute the only one foundation of its beliefs, teachings, life and works."[192] But he adds that the Ecumenical Symbola, *Confessio Augustana* and *Luther's Small Cathechism,* are understood as core summaries of the scriptures. Especially *Luther's Small Catechism* has a strong position and is the basic tool for education in the FLM.

> It is used in all levels of educational teaching: training of Godparents, the first book to be known by heart for the confirmation class and the catechumens, one of the core courses of lay people who want to serve the church as deacons, shepherds and so on, the basic book to be learnt by heart for those who desire to move from a non-Lutheran church to the MLC [FLM], one of the books in the Seminary syllabus. In addition, each newly married couple receives a Bible from their church as a gift, accompanied by a recommendation by the Pastor to read it and make it the favorite book of the family members to guide their lives. The Bible is used in various facets of the Christian education in the MLC [FLM] and in the nurturing of the identity in the branches.[193]

The Lutheran identity is strong but should not be understood as a fence against others but as something good and important which the Lutheran church has and which others can learn from, says Pastor Peri Rasolondraibe. "We have, in a more profound way, understood grace and freedom and our task is to bring this to others. Other denominations have other things that we can learn from," according to him.[194] He continues by saying that the Lutheran identity of the church looks very different depending on who you ask. Among the members there are many different understandings of what it means to be Lutheran. Ask a minister or the leaders of the church and they will give a theological explanation, whereas a common parishioner will give a different answer that probably has something to do

---

192. Randrianasolo, "Malagasy Lutheran Church," 4. UP.
193. Ibid., 4.
194. Rasolondraibe, Peri. Interview.

with belonging to the revival movement.[195] Many members have left their religious background just to join the revival movement which they find in the Lutheran church; they therefore associate revival with Luther.[196] He says that, as a means of educating people in a simple way, in his church they have printed small pamphlets with Luther's basic teaching, so that everyone can have it as a bookmark in their bible or hymn book.[197] President of the FLM, Rakoto Endor Modeste also stresses the church's Lutheran identity. He points out that the FLM is working to deepen its ecumenical relations, but doing so without losing its Lutheran identity.[198] He also tells—just like Peri Rasolondraibe—that the FLM has most of its members in the countryside and many members are very poor. A Lutheran identity is therefore not always very clear to them.[199] While the church's basic identity is Lutheran, it is also in constant transition in order to be what it is meant to be. Moreover, its foundation is that of a mission church and it still largely understands itself as a mission church, trying to reach people with the gospel, winning them for Jesus.[200] The FLM describes its identity and vision, as well as the challenges and obstacles to reaching its vision, as follows:

> VISION:
>
> *The Malagasy Lutheran Church, preaches the Gospel, stands for Christ's witness, progresses in doing good works, develops all the people and the whole being.*
>
> VALUE:
>
> The Malagasy Lutheran Church is based upon the following statements: Faith alone, Holy Scriptures alone, Grace alone.
>
> CHALLENGES:
>
> *Preaching the Gospel*:
>
> To make Christ's disciples of all the Malagasy people and other nations in order to be saved.
>
> To enable one Christian to bring an unbeliever to Jesus.
>
> To make one pastor in charge of one parish.
>
> *Standing for Jesus Christ's witness*:

---

195. Ibid.
196. Ibid.
197. Ibid.
198. Endor Modeste, Rakoto. Interview.
199. Ibid.
200. Randrianasolo, "Malagasy Lutheran Church," 2. UP.

A church that educates its members to be the witnesses of God's truth in society through their words, their ways of life and their works.

A Malagasy Lutheran Church that has its appropriate place within the national and international church federation.

Progressing in doing good works:

A church that gives responsibilities to each Christian for carrying out its task and its self-reliance.

A church that takes care of the management of its self-reliance.

A church that is able to manage with transparence, orderly and normally, its resources, possessions, time and people.

A church that is able to take care of its own workers: wages, equipment, training, retirement.

A church that has a clear relationship and is able to communicate the news all over the Malagasy Lutheran Church fields, the plans and decisions that have been made.

Developing all the people and the whole being:

A church that is able to assist and lead the community towards the improvement of the standard of their living.

A church that is able to exploit its own Christians' talents and skills for development.

A church that is able to take care of the needy and the poor.

A church that is able to make the most of and master the good relationship with the following partners: government, co-worker missionaries, other organizations and so on.[201]

To be able to accomplish what is said in the church's vision and to meet the challenges, the FLM has a widespread work, dealing partly with more explicitly religious themes, partly with more social themes. As said, the Bible and Luther's Small Catechism are important tools to implement what is Christian belief in general and more particularly what is Lutheran belief. But also in its praxis the church tries to implement its Lutheran heritage. Joseph Randrianasolo explains that the Sunday service in the FLM is to a great extent conservative, in the sense of being repetitive. It looks the same from one Sunday to the next.[202] Missionary Arild Bakke says that in many ways it resembles the old Norwegian Sunday service used by the Norwegian missionaries.[203] Some say the service is boring, according to Joseph

---

201. "Malagasy Lutheran Church Vision." UP.
202. Randrianasolo, Joseph. Interview.
203. Bakke, Arild. Interview.

Randrianasolo, but he sees it differently. He wants to see the liturgy as a catechism, something that teaches people what is important, which it does by constant repetition. But he also sees a problem in the lack of enculturation in some aspects of the service. As an example he writes that only western instruments are used; the traditional Malagasy instruments are not allowed to "cross the church's threshold."[204] At the same time, the service is open to the local culture in other ways. Services on special occasions resemble local festivities; on these occasions, the taking of the Lord's Supper is closer to the Malagasy conception of eating together to end a festivity than to the need for forgiveness through justification by faith.[205] Also the length of the service is in accordance with Malagasy traditions. A normal service takes two to three hours, while a service for a special occasion can last from four to six hours. But although much of the Sunday service resembles a traditional service, there are things which are different. Arild Bakke points to the importance of healing in the church. Before, healing was something that occurred in the home; today it is integrated in the service. He also says that demons and healing are important parts of the traditional culture and a lot of people have found something of this in their Christian belief. In that way they combine their traditional culture with Christianity.[206]

The FLM has more than twenty Branches working towards the church's goal, some inside the church, others reaching out to society in general; but they all have the same goal—realizing the FLM as a mission church.

> [T]he MLC [FLM] is predicted to be a church in mission. Its Constitution articulates this in a vivid, dynamic way. The inner working out of its branches prepares its members for that vocation. Training and meetings draw attention to that goal. Christian education fortifies the identity of being part of that organizational church. The role of the Branches consists in doing precisely this. The Branches of the MLC [FLM] are divided in two. On the one hand, seven Branches maintain the Body of Christ and its identity through the inside mission. On the other hand, more than fifteen other Branches do the outreach mission. They practice their work of concretizing the caring love of God in the community. A short devotion attended by their members and some outsiders precedes everyday work.[207]

204. Randrianasolo. "Malagasy Lutheran Church," 6. UP.
205. Ibid.
206. Bakke, Arild. Interview.
207. Randrianasolo, "Malagasy Lutheran Church," 7. UP.

The overall goal of the seven branches concerned with the inside of the church is the proclamation of the Gospel and educating people to be able to be witnesses of their faith. This is seen as the best way of enriching members of the church and fostering future leaders. As an example, Joseph Randrianasolo mentions the Sunday School Branch. Between 50 and 300 children—depending on the size of the congregation—meet for two hours every Sunday, before or after Sunday service. The meetings gather children between the ages of four and sixteen and follow a special program that lasts for 9 years. Each class has its own book, containing bible teaching and confessional writings. Each year ends with an exam.[208]

For the outreaching branches, the FLM has a widespread and well-functioning social work. It runs primary and secondary schools all over the country. It also runs two farm schools and has training programs for peasants. All in all it runs 300 schools, six theological seminaries, twenty Bible schools and a theological faculty. There are also plans for a Lutheran university. The FLM has also had a health department since 1979, running seven hospitals and twenty-five dispensaries. Altogether the church employs ninety physicians and eighteen dental surgeons working with primary care, infant mortality, tuberculosis, leprosy, HIV/AIDS, and other needs.

As mentioned above, the FLM is growing very rapidly. It is said that a new congregation is established almost every week.[209] There are many explanations for this, such as the huge social work and the church's mission, but probably mainly the awakening movement that has spread over Madagascar and the Lutheran church on various occasions in the past century. A majority of Madagascans strongly believe in spirits, demons and exorcism; the awakening movement has done a tremendous amount to forge ties between traditional beliefs and Christianity.[210]

> This situation offers opportunities for lesser gods or the ancestors to serve as intermediaries between the living and the dead. There are bad spirits and good spirits. The bad spirits enjoy inflicting people with suffering and bad luck. The good ones take care of their worshippers through a medium. The bad ones force, Peritheir way to possess people, whereas the good ones are invited to possess someone. Nevertheless, if their demands are not met, the good ones may betray their followers and become bad spirits. Both

---

208. Ibid., 8.
209. Endor Modeste, Rakoto. Interview.
210. Rasolondraibe, Peri. Interview.

the bad and the good impose severe rules and taboos on their worshippers. Power is the name of the game. The ancestors also strive for a place in Madagascan culture. They exert a definitive influence on the lives of Madagascans. The dead attain the status of ancestors when the funeral rituals are all performed in the customary way. This is why Madagascans spend so much money on building a tomb, the processing of which is a matter for the familial circle; members of the family are obliged to contribute. Reburying the dead, *famadihana,* is a *devoir* (a must) for the family to please the ancestors and appease their anger.[211] This is another way for the invisible world of spirits to coerce their followers to strict submission.... We can recognize that the Malagasy world view addresses life in its daily questions and aspirations. Madagascans expect the invisible world to intervene to help them and fulfill them. The active actors and intermediaries in this dynamic process are the ancestors or the spirits of the dead. Sacrifices, various rituals to please or appease the spirits, and possessing spirits are the means to relate to them. They enhance the well-being of their worshippers through healings, blessings, positive answers to petitions and protection. Briefly, they demonstrate that they have the power to distribute health, wealth and benefits. At the heart of the culture there is a hidden but empowering and controlling religion. In fact, we are dealing with a cultural cult.... Syncretism has not been a new factor in the history of the Christian faith in Madagascar. People go to church on Sunday but still practice the traditional cultural cult in times of crisis or for daily needs. It seems to be beyond human power to overcome the obstacle to Christian faith according to the Lutheran teaching. That is true. Only another God endowed with the Highest Power and Authority can overcome it. The history of the *Fifohazana* began with the victory of Jesus Christ over this cultural cult.[212]

Fifohazana

There have been many awakening movements in African countries but most of them have led to tension and eventually split the church, and the awakening movement has formed its own church. Madagascar is an exception. Here the awakening movement has been totally integrated within the

---

211. Reburial of the dead—*famadihana*—is not practiced along the coast. It is a tradition mostly to be found among the Marina and Bara. But respect for the spirits of the dead is to be found all over Madagsacar.

212. Randrianasolo, "Malagasy Lutheran Church," 10-11. UP.

FLM.²¹³ There have been and still can be tensions in Madagascar.²¹⁴ But as Rakoto Endor Modeste says, today the tension is due, not to disapproval of the awakening movement, but to it sometimes being used in the wrong way, as when, for example, people elevate the leader instead of Jesus.²¹⁵ Today Fifohazana is so integrated within the church that you cannot be a pastor in the FLM without approving it. That happened very quickly. The awakening movement was fully accepted in the church in 1975 and by 1984 pastors opposing the movement were contested; today, as mentioned, as an FLM pastor you have to accept it.²¹⁶

> ... the awakening movement has been willing to work within the church. It respects the organization of the church and does not intend to become a separate church on its own. The FLM, on its part, has done well to include in its worship a special liturgy for healing. A healing service is held in each congregation according to local needs. The church has allowed its members to use the gifts God has endowed them. Both the church and the awakening movement are aware that they have the same purpose, the same vision and the same call, which is doing God's mission.²¹⁷

It all began in 1894 during a difficult time for Madagascar: a malaria epidemic, severe famine and the start of French colonization. The awakening movement has then come in waves—1929, 1941, 1946—each of which coincided with a time of struggle.²¹⁸ The first, in 1894, occurred through a witchdoctor, Rainisoalambo. The story goes that he was tormented by a persistent illness from which he was finally cured when he obeyed a vision in which God told him to get rid of his old deities.

> On the evening of October 14, 1894, at 9:00 p.m., he called upon God, whom the missionary had taught him about, and prayed as follows: "O God, what is really the reason for my suffering this much? Forgive me; please heal me. Amen." He then saw light coming from the roof and a man wearing a white robe who looked at him compassionately and said: "Throw away all your fetishes and you'll be healed." He collected right away a whole basket of charms

---

213. Bakke, Arild. Interview.
214. Ibid.
215. Endor Modeste, Rakoto. Interview.
216. Rasolondraibe, Peri. Interview.
217. Ranarivony, "Renewal Movement," 4. UP.
218. Ibid., 1.

and burnt them in the open fire inside the house. He started to feel better. . . . after crying for God's forgiveness throughout the night. God kept his promise and healed him. What a release! Rainisoalambo could not keep this good news to himself. He started to teach others about God; thus becoming a Bible study leader in his house. He had 12 students who together with him made a covenant that a lesson is not learnt until it is applied in daily life. During their usual gathering for prayer and Bible study on June 9, 1895, the house where they met shook. The Holy Spirit came upon them. Rainisoalambo laid his hand on each of them and they agreed (after being empowered) to bearing the name "the lord's disciples or apostles."[219]

Rainisoalambo organized a Christian community, Soatanana Toby, and became its leader. Today it is one of the three major revival centers in the FLM, to which about fifty Tobys are affiliated.[220] A Toby functions as a camp for caring for the sick, mentally ill and demon-possessed. It also functions as a shelter for people who temporarily need one and its goal is to bring people back into society, as researcher Mariette Razivelo explains.[221] The core of the Fifohazana is the office of Shepherd. A Shepherd is a person who has "experienced 'awakening to the power of God', professes faith in the saving work of the Triune God through Jesus Christ and declares willingness to follow Christ in this self-sacrificing ministry of shepherding."[222] The ministry of the Shepherd has its biblical foundations in Acts 6–7, about the seven deacons, set apart to care for the poor but who turned out to be powerful preachers, and Acts 20, about the presbyteros who acted as leaders in the house churches.[223] Peri Rasolondraibe explains:

> My point here is that the shepherd ministry of empowerment is grounded in scripture and the Lord is present in that ministry in his church today. Thus, it does not matter to me what it is called. What is important is that it brings us back to the experience of the early church and forces us to re-examine our established concept of ministry. Christ calls men and women to be shepherds in his church, and he blesses their ministry.[224]

219. Razivelo, "Influences of Awakening," 2. UP.
220. Ibid., 6.
221. Razivelo, Mariette. Interview.
222. Rasolondraibe, "Awakening to the Power of God," 2. UP.
223. Ibid., 10.
224. Ibid.

If this willingness to be a shepherd lasts, she or he (75 percent are women) asks for permission from the pastor to go for training once a week for two years.[225] The shepherd ministry has three parts: God's Word, prayer and diaconia. In praxis it can involve preaching, teaching and counseling, but also intercession and exorcism along with social work. Prayer has a very important position for a shepherd; for instance, every morning in a Toby begins with exorcism and every day ends with exorcism by the shepherd.[226]

> Diaconia work, in towns or cities, may take the form of giving hospitality to strangers, delinquent youth, estranged wives or abused girls seeking asylum, orphans, unwanted babies, mentally disturbed persons, demon-possessed persons, and so on. It may take the form of helping the poor and unemployed find some means of livelihood. This is usually done as group work. Visiting people in prison, in hospitals, the shut-ins.
>
> In a Toby, every shepherd is entrusted with 4 to 5 (sometimes up to 8) patients. The shepherd is expected to provide for all the physical, social and educational needs of her/his patients, in addition to praying for them (with laying on of hands and exorcism) at least three times a day. The patients are cared for as members of her/his own family. She/he does all this without any remuneration apart from the privilege of working side by side with Jesus of Nazareth.[227]

A shepherd can be commissioned to work in a parish or in a Toby; their contribution is a great help to the pastor, and much like a pastor's work.[228] They do most things the pastor does except for celebrating mass and baptisms. They can even be in charge of a congregation and people sometimes call then pastor.[229] The Fifohazana in Madagascar originated in the FLM but has spread to all the major churches. The difference, Peri Rasolondraibe says, is that only in the FLM is it totally integrated. In other churches it is something separate, only for those who are interested. In the FLM the awakening movement is in many ways challenging the entire church, not just part of it.[230]

225. Rasolondraibe, Peri. Interview.
226. Randrianasolo, "Malagasy Lutheran Church," 12. UP.
227. Rasolondraibe, "Awakening to the Power of God," 3. UP.
228. Ranarivony, "Renewal Movement," 3. UP.
229. Rasolondraibe, Peri. Interview.
230. Ibid.

The Fifohazana attracts a lot of people, not least because of what it has in common with the traditional beliefs, in which spirits play an important role, and therefore it has also influenced services in the FLM. Depending on the size of the congregation, there is often more than one service every Sunday and it often consists of two parts; the first—up to the offering—is a traditional service, while the second includes communion, confirmation or a session that centers on the awakening movement, with prayer, laying on of hands, exorcism and so on.[231] One difference from, for example, the Neo-Pentecostal movement is that in the Fifohazana weeping takes the place of clapping of hands, shouting and so on.[232] Besides the Sunday service, Fifohazana services are often held in the morning on weekdays, in some congregations once a week, in others six days a week. They are normally structured to include one or two sermons, laying on of hands, prayer and exorcism.[233]

The Fifohazana has also affected the role of laypeople in the church. The central office in the FLM is that of pastor—there is no bishop, but a president—but the creation of the office of shepherds has made the church considerably more open to people who say they are called by God without being a minister. As a shepherd they have room in the church to work and preach. Peri Rasolondraibe means that in doing this, the FLM practices Luther's doctrine of the Universal Priesthood.

> The doctrine of the Priesthood of all believers, much cherished by Lutherans, has in fact taken concrete possibilities and expressions through the Awakening movement. The church is the people of God (not the bishops or the clergies) gathered around the Word and Sacraments (CA 7) and sent out into the world with the grace and power God bestowed on them through these means of grace. The Fifohazana sees the church in terms of an organism rather than as an organization with rigid structures. This way of being the church, not simply attending church, is highly appreciated by people as God-sent.[234]

He also means that the centrality of the Word and the understanding of justification by grace through faith which is to be found in the awakening

---

231. Ibid.
232. Razivelo, "Influences of Awakening" 6. UP.
233. Ibid.
234. Rasolondraibe, "Awakening to the Power of God," 9. UP.

movement, in many ways correspond with central ideas of Luther. In that way, the Fifohazana has helped to improve the church's Lutheran identity.[235]

Women's Situation

The situation of women is changing in Madagascar, both in society in general and in the church. Traditionally, Madagascan society is patriarchal. Tribes have had their own traditions but in general they have all seen women as different from men. Coastal tribes have always tended to neglect women more than tribes in the highland; that is still the case but becoming less so. Researcher Lotera Fabien says that in traditional Madagascan society, women have never had an official role except for the queen in Antananarivo. In a divorce, women were not allowed to take anything with them. If a man died, his wife did not necessarily inherit anything. Polygamy has been normal in some parts of the country, but never for women. Education has been men's privilege; women have waited at home to get married and so on. All in all, the situation for women has been, and still is, hard, though this is changing.[236]

Change today is rapid in the cities. Women go to schools and universities, earn the same salaries as men and can have whatever occupation they like. This is also happening in rural areas but is taking longer.[237] In the church, however, things seem to be changing more slowly than in the rest of society. Women do not hold any of the higher posts in the church. And although the church is mostly made up of women, there are few women in the synods and there they are mostly silent.[238]

> All the heads of the 23 synods of the FLM are men. From the beginning of the FLM up to the present day, presidents of the church have been men. No woman has been elected president of the synod . . . The majority of people serving in councils within the FLM are men. Few women are serving on church councils though the majority of church membership is composed of women. It is worth mentioning that women serving on councils remain silent during the meetings. Only a few could participate in the committees' discussions. This long silence of women during Church

---

235. Ibid.
236. Fabien, Lotera. Interview.
237. Rasolondraibe, Peri. Interview.
238. Ibid.

gatherings reflects Malagasy culture: women must remain silent in front of men, otherwise they will be likened to hens cackling.[239]

Women in the FLM are to be found as regular churchgoers, in deacon ministry and as shepherds, but not as pastors or leaders of the church. Peri Rasolondraibe says that the issue of women's ordination has been on and off the church's agenda ever since 1976. In that year the church wrote that there are no biblical obstacles, and no obstacles in tradition. It is all in the culture. But nothing has happened since then.[240] He goes on to ask why women elect conservative men to the councils. Women have 80 percent of the votes; if they used them in favor of women, things could change rapidly. But he concludes by saying that a woman would never go against her husband. Rakoto Endor Modeste considers that the church really has worked on the issue of women's ordination, even as recently as in 2008. Opinions differ, he says, but the matter has always been voted down in the synods because the church is not yet ready. He adds that this does not seem to be a big issue in Madagascar, not even among women; "we have more urgent questions to deal with." He concludes by saying that the issue is largely imposed by countries in the west.[241]

Women have been allowed to enter theological schools since 1974. Today they make up 40 percent of every class, which means that about 200 women in the FLM have a theological training. That is largely a consequence of the LWF's regulations, which make financial support conditional on 40 percent being women.

> Before 1974, women were not allowed to enter theological schools. Things changed in the 70s, so from 1974 the MLC [FLM] decided to permit young women to attend the seminaries. Women were given an equal opportunity with men. Both males and females have been allowed to get training and education in the theological schools. Some synods were not willing at first—and even these days—to allow young women to enter seminaries. The LWF requires that 40 percent of the students recruited to study at SALT must be women. The LWF withholds the scholarship grant for a class if this requirement is not respected. Therefore SALT makes sure that each time we recruit new students, 40 percent of them

---

239. Fabien, "Women's Situation," 5. UP.
240. Rasolondraibe, Peri. Interview.
241. Endor Modeste, Rakoto. Interview.

are women. This provides good opportunities for young women to study theology.²⁴²

This is both good and bad. The good thing is that they are educated and the bad that they cannot get a job. Rakoto Endor Modeste concludes that the LWF is trying to impose its values on the FLM, even though the FLM is not ready. Others see the frustration of women in the FLM.

> At their graduation, women theological students are given diplomas or degrees such as licentiates and master degrees. At this level they are equal to male theological students. But quite a number of women theological students, after the completion of their studies, suffer discrimination by their respective synods. The synods appoint only male candidates to different posts, but do not find any post to give to women candidates. Most of the male candidates are consecrated to pastoral ministry, which means they get ordained, but female candidates are unfortunately not ordained. Ordination is the right of male candidates and is not allowed for female candidates. So within the FLM they are only called as theologians. They are not called as pastors. . . . This situation of women theologians in the FLM is highly frustrating for female candidates and causes heated debates.²⁴³

Women's issues are important for many in the church, be it women's rights in society in general or women's ordination. But the church is divided, at least when it comes to ordination, and so far the church is said to lag behind society in general in this particular question.²⁴⁴

Structure and Leadership

As said, the FLM is a church predominantly made up of women but led by men. However, there are important exceptions. In the Fifohazana, most of the leaders have been women, both as shepherds and as leaders in the movement. Arild Bakke especially mentiones Volahavana Germaine, or Nenilava, as a person of tremendous importance for the church. Her ministry began in 1941 and lasted until her death in 1998.²⁴⁵ During that time she established more than fifty Tobys, always using Matt 10:8—you receive

---

242. Fabien, "Women's Situation," 5. UP.
243. Ibid.
244. Rasolondraibe, Peri. Interview.
245. Bakke, Arild. Interview.

freely; give freely—as her guideline.[246] But outside the Fifohazana, male domination is massive.

The FLM has around 5000 congregations. Normally a pastor has between one and six churches to attend to. Together they form a parish. The churches meet every other month for discussion, training and so on. About five parishes make up a district, led by a district president. The parishes in the district meet every three months for deliberations. A synod contains five or more districts and is led by a president of the synod. It meets once a year. Today there are about twenty-three synods in the FLM and together they form the Great Synod, which meets every fourth year for discussions of importance for the future of the FLM.[247]

An important task for the leaders of the church is to maintain the FLM's status as a Lutheran church. It is growing very fast and there are some similarities with traditional Malagasy culture, which could affect its identity. Rakoto Endor Modeste says that if, for example, a person says he is a prophet, it is important that the leaders decide whether or not he is a true prophet. It is very important to be strict and not let the traditional religious culture enter the church, disguised as something Lutheran.[248]

Arild Bakke means that, particularly after the military coup, there are huge problems in society in general. Corruption is widespread and those with money can buy almost everything. Politicians are being imprisoned. Most people are becoming poorer. During the recent years of political unrest in Madagascar the church has been very quiet, not only about political issues, but also on ethical and moral questions. In the future, he says, he hopes the FLM can remain neutral when it comes to politics but also that it will have a stronger prophetic voice in society in general.[249]

Summary

The FLM is growing rapidly. One of many reasons for this is that the church forms a community of people who take care of each other. As a member of the FLM you get access to a community that sees you and takes care of you. But perhaps the most influential aspect of the FLM is the Fifohazana, a movement whereby the FLM has succeeded in combining the traditional culture with what it sees as a good expression of Christian faith in the

246. Rasolondraibe. "Awakening to the Power of God," 2. UP.
247. Randrianasolo, "Malagasy Lutheran Church," 7. UP.
248. Endor Modeste, Rakoto. Interview.
249. Bakke, "Programrapport fra Representant, 2010." UP.

context of Madagascar. Most people seem to be convinced that the Fifohazana is a major reason for the FLM's rapid growth.

Many aspects of the FLM have been formed by the two churches that shaped it from the beginning. The way to celebrate Sunday service and many other things in the FLM are unmistakably legacies from those churches. Some of the ethical or moral codes that are to be found in the FLM could also be related to former codes in the founding churches. But that is not the whole picture; the FLM is also a church that seeks renewal in many ways. Perhaps the most striking is how the old liturgy in the Sunday service is combined with a revivalist movement that emphasizes other aspects than what is traditional.

According to its vision, the FLM is a church that wants to see itself as a servant of people. They spread the gospel through social work as well as by religious education and services. The members experience a church which tries to meet the whole person, body and soul, in all that it is doing.

INDONESIA—HURIA KRISTEN BATAK PROTESTAN, HKBP

Indonesia is the world's fourth largest country, with 245 million inhabitants.[250] They live on more than 18,000 islands spread over 5000 kilometers from east to west and 2000 kilometers from north to south.

Most Indonesians are descendants of Malay people who came from India, Cambodia, Vietnam and China between 5000 and 2500 years ago. They founded small kingdoms which eventually became so prosperous that they were important trading partners for India. In that way, Hinduism found its way to Indonesia. The Hindu Majapahit Empire started to spread rapidly in 1294 and soon controlled most of the larger islands. In the fifteenth century the Majapahit fled to Bali and Islamic rulers took over. In the next few centuries the region was in turmoil as the Portuguese, Spanish, Dutch, and British tried to gain control of the islands. A major factor in this struggle was the powerful Dutch East India Company (1602–1799). In the end, Indonesia became a Dutch colony in 1800 and remained so (with a short British interval) until the Japanese invasion during World War II. The

---

250. The text is mainly built on interviews and unprinted sources. The interviews are marked "interviews" in the footnotes and the informants' names are given in the footnotes. The informants are listed in the bibliography under the heading "Interviews". The unprinted sources are marked "UP" in the footnotes and are listed in the bibliography under the heading "Unprinted sources".

The brief introductions to the countries are not footnoted; the information there is general knowledge, easily accessed in any guidebook.

Japanese were considered harsh rulers but they did allow Indonesian people to work in government and made Bahasa Indonesia the official language.

After Japan's capitulation, there were some years of fighting with the British and the Dutch before Indonesia proclaimed its independence in 1945 and the Dutch recognized its sovereignty in 1949. The freedom-fighter Sukarno became the first president and launched a long period of non-democratic regimes, just as before. Sukarno talked of a "third way" between communism and capitalism but leaned on the Soviet Union and China. When seven high ranking officers were murdered in 1965, the army blamed the Communists; between 100,000 and 2000,000 people died in the ensuing riots and violence. Another officer, Suharto, took over and during his regime, 1968–98, Indonesia developed into a strong military force as well as an important economy in the international market. By the end of Suharto's rule, however, the economy was in ruins, which led to demonstrations and riots, and he was forced to leave the presidency. Since then, Indonesia has moved towards democracy, with free presidential elections in 1999, 2004, and 2009.

Today Indonesia is a democracy with a relatively stable economy but has huge problems with poverty, corruption and, not least, environmental damage. The economy is based on rich natural resources, such as oil, minerals and natural gas. Fishing, farming and the vast forests are also important. Nevertheless, about a third of the population lives in poverty, mainly in rural areas, and unemployment is high. A 9-year education is compulsory and about 60 percent complete it. There are many universities and many young people go on to higher education.

There are approximately 400 ethnic groups in Indonesia, most of them with their own language. Bahasa Indonesia, the ancient trading language, serves as the lingua franca. 87 percent of the population is Muslim, which makes Indonesia the world's largest Muslim country. There are also Christians, Hindus, Buddhists, Confucians, and believers in traditional religions. Traditionally, the different religious and ethnic groups have lived side by side in peace. But in some parts of the country there have been frequent uprisings and clashes between groups and religions, due in part to migration, in part to small fundamentalist Muslim groups that have recently started to spread.

Indonesia is a religious country; every Indonesian man and woman is required by law to have a religion. This is the home of many churches, of which one is among the world's largest Lutheran churches, Huria Kristen Batak Protestan (HKBP).

Foundation of the Church

British and American missionaries arrived in north Sumatra in the early nineteenth century. Nothing much happened for the first 40 years, but in 1861 the first Bataks were baptized by Dutch missionaries. When a German missionary, Ludwig Nommensen, from the Rheinische Missions-Gesselschaft (RMG), arrived in the following year, things started to change. A seminary for teachers opened in 1877, followed by a seminary for preachers in 1884. Nommensen was elected "Ephorus" or bishop by the Batak congregations in 1881. In 1930 the HKBP became the first independent church in the Dutch colony and it has been a member of the LWF since 1952.[251] For various reasons, some cultural, others doctrinal, over the years there have been numerous splits within the HKBP. Still, today the HKBP is the third largest Christian group in Indonesia after the Roman Catholic and Pentecostal churches. It is to be found in many parts of the country but its main center is in the Batak region in northern Sumatra.[252]

Becoming a Lutheran church was not a straightforward matter for the HKBP. With its roots in the Rheinische Missions-Gesellschaft, says church official Binsar Nainggolan, it introduced itself as belonging to the Church of Westphalia, which is a *Uniert* church of three parts: Lutheran, Reformed, and United. "So for the first 90 years we were not Lutheran," he says. However, after the Japanese invasion during World War II and the end of the war against the Dutch, in the late 1940s and early 1950s the economic situation was troublesome and the HKBP wanted to join a larger organization.[253] In 1950 an application for membership of the LWF was turned down because, Binsar Nainggolan says, the church did not use the Lutheran confessional texts. After some time, the LWF sent a representative to Indonesia who found that they did use Luther's Small Catechism along with the Heidelberg Catechism from the Reformed tradition, as well as other Lutheran confessional writings. After discussions and the formulation in 1951 of its own confession, strongly influenced by the Augsburg Confession, the HKBP was accepted as a member of the LWF.[254] The 1951 confession contains

251. Nainggolan, Binsar. Interview.
252. Aritonang, Jan. Interview.
253. Nainggolan, Binsar. Interview.
254. Ibid.

eighteen articles concerning God, the Trinity, the Special Act of the Triune God, the Word of God, Origin of Sin, Inherited Sin, Salvation from Sin, the Church, Those who minister in the Church, the Holy sacraments, the Church Order, Government of the State, Sunday, Food, Faith and Good Works, remembrance of the Dead, the Angels, and the Last Judgment. Each article ends with a formulation of opposition and rejection: "By means of this doctrine we oppose..."[255] A preface to the articles states that,

> Because of pressures upon the church from every side, we must at this time arouse our thinking to confront the religions and teachings around us. Formerly there were only two religions around us, heathenism and Islam. At the present time, however, there are many, those which come from without and also those which have grown up from within. We name them one by one:[256]

This is followed by a list of religious groups and a short explanation of each. It starts with Roman Catholics and the comment "[n]ow this group comes once again to spread its wings. Our doctrine is in opposition to its teaching."[257] After the Roman Catholics come Adventists, Pentecostals, Enthusiasts, Si Raja Batak, The Bible-Circle Group, Nationalistic Christianity, Syncretism, Heathenism and Islam.[258] It ends by noting that "[t]here are other dangerous movements and doctrines which threaten the church, for example, the doctrines that come from Theosophy, Communism and Capitalism."[259] After a process that began in 1987, a new confession was adopted in 1996, similar in many ways but adapted to the present context of Indonesia by including articles regarding human beings, society, culture and environment. Moreover, it does not include either the preface or the list of things to which the HKBP is opposed.[260]

Today the HKBP understands itself as a Lutheran church and is a member of the LWF. It is headed by an Ephorus or bishop and a secretary general. Under them are twenty-six districts led by twenty-six praeses, with a total of 3017 parishes. There are 1300 ordained pastors, 400 teacher-preachers, 400 Bible Women and more than 200 deaconesses. They all lead services and most other activities in the church, but only the pastors

---

255. Aritonang, "Some Notes on the Confession of HKBP." UP.
256. Ibid.
257. Ibid.
258. Ibid.
259. Ibid.
260. Ibid.

administer the sacraments and perform matrimony. A majority of the members are from poor rural areas and work as farmers; however, approximately 30 percent live in cities and have highly qualified jobs. On the World Council of Churches website the HKBP presents itself as follows:

> The HKBP understands itself as a church of Christ, established by the work of the Holy Spirit, an organism that "lives from age to age and from generation to generation across the borders of continents, nations, races and languages." It is part of the universal church, holding to one baptism. It has its own confession, adopted in 1951, which is based on the Holy Scriptures, on the Apostles', Nicene and Athanasian creeds, the Reformation and more recent confessions like the Barmen Theological Declaration of 1934. According to the latest revision of its constitution, the HKBP has a vision of developing itself to be an inclusive, dialogical and transparent church that, together with other Christians and people of other faiths, strives for the improvement of the quality of life of the people in the light of the love of Jesus Christ, for the glory of God. The mission of the church is carried out through its three departments: Diakonia, Marturia and Koinonia. The main concerns are bringing the gospel to non-Christian people (e.g., among Javanese and Tamil in Medan, tribes in Riau, in areas of transmigration), providing social services (e.g., care for orphans, for the blind, for drop-outs), gender justice, schools (nursery, elementary, high schools and technical, 145 in all), hospitals and health centers, HIV/AIDS, environment, violence and poverty. An important institution of the HKBP is the Nommensen University, which was opened in 1954 in response to the felt need for higher education in the new nation of Indonesia.[261]

As indicated above, the HKBP has a huge work among its members that also reaches out to non-members and society in general. The Orphanage plays an important role, particularly during the unrest in Aceh province. The schools operated by the church are also becoming increasingly important as the economy develops. The Nommensen University, run by the HKBP, is the largest Lutheran university in the world, with 9000 students and programs in agriculture, economics, education, business administration, engineering, arts and languages. The HKBP also runs two large hospitals, one on the mainland and one on an island in Lake Toba. There is also a huge youth organization working with various projects. As a church with most of its members from rural areas, the HKBP runs major rural

261. "Protestant Christian Batak Church."

community development programs.²⁶² All in all, the HKBP is a huge church with a widespread work among members and non-members, but also a church facing many difficult challenges. Two main issues in the future are, according to researcher Darwin Lumbantobing, the country's radically heterogeneous culture with a predominantly Muslim population—how to be a church in such a situation—and how to deal meaningfully with poverty and other social questions.²⁶³

At the same time as the HKBP presents itself as a Lutheran church with much social work and pathos, it is also in some ways a church struggling to find out what it means to be a Lutheran church in Indonesia today. It was only fairly recently that the Lutheran confessional texts were translated in full into Indonesian; the translation of the Book of Concord was completed in 2004.²⁶⁴ During the last thirty years the HKBP has had more frequent exchanges with other large Lutheran churches such as the Evangelical Lutheran Church in America (ELCA) and the Lutheran Church of Australia (LCA).²⁶⁵ Both the translation of the confessional texts and this developed exchange have been important for the construction of the HKBP's identity and are gradually making this and especially the Lutheran identity more solid, according to Darwin Lumbantobing.²⁶⁶ The interest in, and knowledge of, Luther and Lutheran identity are steadily growing at the same time as the HKBP is constructing its own way of being Lutheran in its Indonesian context. Researcher Jan Aritonang discerns eleven main characteristics of the Lutheran churches in Indonesia:

> Based on the teaching of Martin Luther, esp. in his Catechism, the Lutheran churches in Indonesia give special attention and emphasis to the Apostolic Creed (*Symbolum Apostolicum*), the Ten Commandments, the "Our Father Prayer" (*Paternoster*), and the two Sacraments (Holy Baptism and Holy Supper).
>
> The doctrine of justification by faith (including *sola fide* and *sola gratia*) is also emphasized in line with the balance of emphasis on the persons of the triune God.
>
> Especially on Baptism, the Lutheran churches in Indonesia practice infant baptism by pouring or sprinkling water (although they also practice adult baptism for new believers).

262. Nainggolan, Binsar. Interview.
263. Lumbantobing, Darwin. Interview.
264. Lumbantobing, "Burning Issues in the Lutheran Church in Indonesia," 2. UP.
265. Ibid.
266. Ibid.

Referring to one of Luther's most important teachings, the Lutheran churches in Indonesia also emphasize justification by faith. But this is also combined or mixed with the importance of applying the Ten Commandments and church discipline, esp. concerning the seventh commandment (sexual conduct/adultery), as an implementation of sanctification.

Concerning the teaching on the Holy Spirit, the Lutheran churches follow the classical Trinitarian doctrine. Therefore there is no special emphasis on the role, works and gifts of the Holy Spirit (e.g., the special charisma and the baptism of the Holy Spirit).

Following the *Uniert* tradition from Germany, the liturgy (order of worship) among the Lutheran churches in Indonesia follows the *Agenda,* which is a product of the 19th century (although some churches have made some modifications or provide some other models). This makes the worship very well-ordered (not to say rigid and formalistic). The elements of liturgy: *Votum, Introitus,* Prayer (after *Introitus*), prayer of confession of sin, prayer for offering, and [intercession] prayer on special days such as Advent, Christmas, New Year, Good Friday, Easter, Ascension, Pentecost, (etc., are already formulated and provided); those who lead worship (the liturgists) cannot express them spontaneously in their own words.

As emphasized by Luther, the center of the worship is proclamation of the gospel or preaching the Word of God. The hymns of praise are also understood and practiced as part of the preaching of the Word. The sermon must be textual-biblical and based on a deep exegesis or interpretation, although also open to contextual and actual illustrations.

For the Lutheran churches in Indonesia—apparently influenced by the Calvinist element in the *Uniert* heritage—Church Order and organization are very important. A lot of time and energy are spent on this and a lot of internal conflicts and even schisms are caused by it.

Church buildings as sanctuaries are also important. Many of the buildings adopt or imitate Western architecture, though some churches also have a number of buildings with traditional-contextual architecture.

Related to the close attention to the Church Order, the Lutheran churches in Indonesia apply the synodal-episcopal model of church polity. The Synod Assembly is the organization's supreme body, followed by the leader of the church (Ephorus or Bishop), although he/she is accompanied and assisted by other organs or functionaries (Secretary General, Heads of Department, Synod Council, etc.).

As a consequence of this model, most of the leaders and decision-makers are senior persons. The young people are viewed and treated as figurants or "flowers of the church" (decoration, accessories).[267]

In describing the situation in the HKBP, Jan Aritonang notes the importance of the Lutheran tradition but also sees influences from Calvinist tradition. Moreover, he stresses the importance of how the faith is made visible, not only in church buildings, liturgy and sermons, but also by emphasizing the Christian life and morals. When it comes to current developments in the HKPB, he points to a few main factors: the rise of Charismatic movements, the HKBP's presence in a society with a Muslim majority, and the interaction of traditional culture and religion.[268]

The Influence of Charismatic Movements

Darwin Lumbantobing writes that even though Lutheran churches in Indonesia had had a heritage of pietism from the very beginning, stemming from the missionaries who brought Christianity to Indonesia, that pietism is very different from what is now happening as Charismatic movements grow inside the Lutheran churches.[269] According to Jan Aritonang, this started about forty years ago when the first Charismatic movements reached Indonesia from the USA. These movements are not confined to a particular denomination. They showed up first in Indonesian's Pentecostal, spread to other, similar churches and then gradually "penetrated and influenced the 'mainline' or 'traditional' churches, incl. the so-called Lutheran churches."[270] Today, a Charismatic movement is to be found in most of the Christian churches in Indonesia; the HKBP is no exception.

Today there are over one hundred Charismatic church organizations in Indonesia. The vast majority of their members are previous members of some of the mainline churches, of which for various reasons they tired, says Jan Aritonang.[271] Quite a few of the HKBP's members—both men and women and younger and older—have joined or started to celebrate ser-

---

267. Aritonang, "Influence and Impact of Charismatic Movements," 1-2. UP.
268. Aritonang, Jan. Interview.
269. Lumbantobing, "Burning Issues in the Lutheran Church in Indonesia," 3. UP.
270. Aritonang, "Influence and Impact of Charismatic Movements," 1. UP.
271. Aritonang, Jan. Interview.

vice in more Charismatic churches; most of them continue to belong to the HKBP, holding a dual membership. And some of them have recently been leaving the Charismatic churches to return to the HKBP, according to Binsar Nainggolan.[272] He also points out that one reason for this is that the HKBP has set about changing itself to cope with the fact that people were leaving for Charismatic churches. What has been adapted, he says, is not in the first place theology but the way services are celebrated. This has traditionally been very strict, with much the same ritual as in the days of the first missionaries.[273]

> The churches are following the German liturgical tradition. They are following an *Agenda* which is a product of the 19th century. It is interesting that this agenda has been dropped in Germany but here in Indonesia we adhere to it very closely and faithfully as if it were the order of worship in heaven. That makes it very hard to renew and change in it.[274]

There is a tendency to stay with the traditional Agenda but many parishes have felt they must do something to counter the loss of members to the Charismatic movements. To this end they have started to hold a second service on Sundays that is in many ways influenced by the Charismatic movements.[275] Examples are having music that differs from the traditional hymns, letting bands play in the church and preaching differently. Instead of reading the sermon, the preacher is much freer; he or she can shout or try to get the congregation to respond in various ways. Many preachers try to imitate the style of pastors in the Charismatic movements.[276] These changes have proved to be a good way of getting members to stay in or return to the HKBP, Binsar Nainggolan says, but other questions remain to be solved. People who have been in contact with a Charismatic movement and come back to the HKBP sometimes bring with them a theology that differs from the traditional HKBP version.[277] Jan Aritonang develops Binsar Nainggolan's thoughts:

---

272. Nainggolan, Binsar. Interview.
273. Ibid.
274. Aritonang, Jan. Interview.
275. Nainggolan, Binsar. Interview.
276. Aritonang, Jan. Interview.
277. Nainggolan, Binsar. Interview.

> Since the main attention and emphasis in Charismatic movements is the Holy Spirit—the being and personality, the works, the blessings, and the fruits—those from the mainstream churches who participate in this movement also pay more attention to and respect pneumatology rather than Christology. The personal and communal experience of the presence of the power of the Holy Spirit is testified more and more.

The function and role of the Holy Spirit are understood more in terms of renewing personal and spiritual life than in renewing or transforming social-political-cultural life. So for members of the mainstream churches who have been influenced by this Charismatic spirituality, involvement and participation in the social-political activities are not important.[278]

There is a shift from Christ to the Holy Spirit which entails a shift from the common good to the individual, which finally leads to a shift from the political to individual salvation.[279] This, says Binsar Nainggolan, the HKBP tries to oppose with various kinds of work, not least social work on a large scale. The HKBP's diaconal unit works both with direct help in times of crisis and with more long-term solutions for problems such as poverty. Education for farmers is one example; others are schools, universities and hospitals.[280]

There are other things in the HKBP that are being done in a new way. Nowadays many people want a different approach to Bible studies. There is a new interest in the Bible, not so much to study it in the traditional or academic way as to read and learn from it. According to Jan Aritonang, a new Bible fundamentalism is to be seen in the church and there is also an increase in spiritual healing, miracles, prophesy and baptism of the Spirit.[281] Binsar Nainggolan also sees this but considers that on the whole it is not very widespread in the HKBP; instead he stresses that the church had to handle the situation with Charismatic movements in the way it did so as not to lose too many members. The task today is to be open to change but continue in the right direction.[282] One way to do that is to develop the

---

278. Aritonang. "Influence and Impact of Charismatic Movements," 3. UP.
279. Aritonang, Jan. Interview.
280. Nainggolan, Binsar. Interview.
281. Aritonang. "Influence and Impact of Charismatic Movements," 4. UP.
282. Nainggolan, Binsar. Interview.

community with other Lutheran churches around the world, which, as previously mentioned, the HKBP is doing.[283]

Church and Culture

As always, there is a relationship between religion and culture. The HKBP has its foundation in Batak culture. Almost all its members are ethnic Bataks and Batak traditions play a special role in the HKBP.

> Generally, Lutheran churches in Indonesia have a close relationship with the local culture. The local congregations are almost all formed from an ethnic group. For instance, HKBP congregations, GKPI congregations, and HKI congregations almost all come from Batak Toba ethnic groups. Almost all GKPS congregations come from Simalungun and almost all GKPA congregations come from Batak Angkola ethnic groups. . . . So, although they do not admit it, Lutheran churches in Indonesia are ethnic churches. Hence their existence and theology are very close to and greatly influenced by the local culture. Even the problems and challenges of the local churches are dominated by their local culture. As a result, the local culture influences life in the church . . .[284]

In the early days of the Batak church, Nommensen tried to separate the Gospel from the traditional Batak culture. The latter was something to get rid of. He soon changed his mind and tried instead to Christianize whatever there was in the culture which he thought could be Christianized and get rid of whatever could not. In that way, Batak culture and the Gospel could meet to some extent.[285] The HKBP has continued along those lines. Binsar Nainggolan says there is a program for retaining those aspects of the culture that do not contradict the Gospel; but if they do contradict the Gospel, there is no room for them in the HKBP. He mentions weddings as an example of a cultural event that has been Christianized. A couple who are getting married today first have the wedding service in the church, but instead of a party afterwards in a restaurant, they have a traditional Batak wedding party, inserted in a Christian framework. One of the most prominent Batak symbols is the *Ulos*, a beautiful piece of cloth with various uses, among which is a gift to a newly wedded couple. Traditionally, the Ulos is

---

283. Lumbantobing, "Burning Issues in the Lutheran Church in Indonesia," 2. UP.
284. Ibid., 1.
285. Nainggolan, Binsar. Interview.

said to have *Mana, sahala,* or power; today the church teaches that the Ulos is a symbol of God's blessing.[286]

Binsar Nainggolan also notes that while the HKBP is doing all it can to preach the Gospel, it is important to remember that it lives in its own context and therefore includes many things that have more to do with culture. But this is as it should be, this is to be contextual. The HKBP is a Batak church and thereby influenced by Batak culture.[287]

A Muslim Majority Society

Indonesia is the world's largest Muslim country with just a small minority of Christians. Moreover, Christianity and Islam are both religions that try to avoid mixing with other religions in order to preserve their doctrine, according to Darwin Lumbantobing.

> Both Islamic and Christian religions are very strict about maintaining and preserving their teachings so that it will not be seen as syncretistic. Therefore these two great religions always work on how to keep their teaching pure, not mixed up with or contaminated by the teachings of other religion and beliefs.... This raises the very interesting question: How are we to live among followers of different religions?
>
> As church doctrine and church congregation must be firm in order to maintain doctrinal purity, faith formulations cannot be compromised. Nevertheless, in social life, church and congregation must build relationships with the whole of society and with members of other religions. Therefore, though our belief is exclusive, our social relations with the rest of society must be inclusive.[288]

Relations between Islam and Christianity have been good and prosperous in the past and still are today but there are signs of changes. Darwin Lumbantobing says that most people in Indonesia know that it is the world's largest Muslim country and they want that to be seen in different ways. Today, legislation is to a large extent Muslim. There are twenty-seven districts that have Sharia laws. He also says that it could be hard for non-Muslims to get a job as a government official. Of course, he adds, this is due

---

286. Ibid.

287. Ibid.

288. Lumbantobing, "Burning Issues in the Lutheran Church in Indonesia," 10-11. UP.

to praxis, not to legislation. Moreover, converting from Islam to any other religion, including Christianity, is strictly forbidden. But doing it the other way round is not a problem.[289] The situation is getting tougher, he says. One explanation lies in the advance of democracy. The government is no longer in absolute control, which is a good thing but makes things harder for Christians as a minority. People can do what they like in the name of democracy, he says. But he adds that this harder situation only applies in some parts of the country, not everywhere.[290]

Lately there have been more serious clashes between Muslims and Christians. Churches have been closed and some time ago one was burned down, says Binsar Nainggolan. He cannot say why this was done but as the church had been there for forty years without causing any problems, he thinks it was not due to a specific religious conflict. Had that been the case, it would not have been possible to build the church in the first place. A more likely explanation is conflicts in the local society. He really wants to stress that the HKBP's most important task today is to be a positive factor in the growing tensions between Islam and Christianity. It is of the utmost importance that education in reconciliation and peaceful living is provided both for members of our church and for the general public. He mentions that the HKBP has set about inviting Muslim leaders to discuss with the Ephorus or bishop in university settings, so that young people can see and hear leaders of the two religions discussing in a friendly and constructive way.[291]

Women's Situation

Women in northern Sumatra, including those who are active in the HKBP, often seem to be second-class citizens compared to men. Researcher Erlina Pardede quotes various results of research to show that women are often exposed to injustice and violence.[292]

> Being beaten and slapped by her husband, with his bare hands or with a broom or utensil, is the most common form of violence experienced by women. The violence is usually directed at the head and face, the eye or cheek. Violence also takes the form of a kick or the destruction of household tools. . . . For women in Dolok

289. Lumbantobing, Darwin. Interview.
290. Ibid.
291. Nainggolan, Binsar. Interview.
292. Pardede, Erlina. Interview.

Sanggul Toba, verbal harassment by the husband is common, for instance expressions such as "sip ma ho, ndang diboto ho manang aha!" (Shut up, you don't know anything). Such treatment generally occurs when a wife expresses an opinion that differs from her husband's.

There are many instances of Toba women being "dipaajarhon" (sent back to their parents' house). The parents are requested to teach their daughter more about how to be a good wife; she can come back when she has finished "her education." Repatriation of a wife usually occurs when, according to her husband, she cannot manage money properly, cannot educate the children, or other things...

Another form of violence is forced sexual intercourse; the wife must be willing at all times, willing to serve whenever the husband wants. Women in rural areas seldom expect understanding from their husbands. Working in the fields all day and at home tires them out. In Dolok Sanggul and the surrounding countryside there are many cases of husbands having an affair with another woman. The same applies when husbands migrate to find work and marry another woman there. If the wife does not agree to all this, she is in danger of being divorced.[293]

These injustices are frequent according to Erlina Pardede and have their roots in the Batak culture.[294] Traditionally, Batak women are marginalized in general, they are not prioritized when it comes to education, they have a larger workload and are exposed to domestic violence.[295] At the same time as she sees a lot of problems in northern Sumatra with issues concerning women, she also realizes that tools are to be found in the Christian tradition and the Bible which can be a help. Traditionally, most people and churches read the Bible from a male perspective, but she says there are other ways of reading the texts. The problem is that the church leaders are fostered in traditional Batak culture and therefore do not clearly see what is happening and go on reading in the traditional way, she says. At the same time she admits that the situation is much better inside the church than outside. The church is doing something to change what is happening, but not enough.[296] One reason for this is that in their praxis, the HKBP together with the other Lutheran churches in Indonesia are not democratic. There

---

293. Pardede, "Women in North Sumatra," 9–10. UP.
294. Pardede, Erlina. Interview.
295. Pardede, "Women in North Sumatra," 5. UP.
296. Pardede, Erlina. Interview.

is a clear order from the top down, with a hierarchy that in many ways resembles the hierarchy between men and women, says Janri Damanik, who is employed by LWF in Medan. He also points out that the churches in Sumatra are in many ways middle-class churches, even though most of their members are poor. The poor hardly ever come to the churches or services, so they do not hear what is said about relations between men and women, when something is said.[297] Another problem is that these issues do not interest the younger middle-class generation; they think that most problems are to be found among the poor and do not concern them.[298]

Today approximately 20 to 30 percent of the pastors are female. The first woman pastor was ordained in 1986. But women still have difficulty in obtaining higher positions. Erlina Pardede means that this matter is complex: while it has been very difficult for women to be elected to higher posts, it has also been hard to find women who are willing to take the responsibility.[299] The first election of a woman as district superintendent or praeses in one of the HKBP's twenty-six districts occurred in 2008.[300]

Summary

The situation is changing for every church in Indonesia. What was previously a functioning—even though it was constructed or forced by a suppressing regime—relationship between a majority Muslim population and a Christian minority is now changing and no one really knows where it will end. This situation has led the HKBP to concentrate more on its own situation.

The HKBP could be described as an ethnic church. In essence it is a church for the Batak people, with a strong hold on northern Sumatra. Today this is neither strange nor a syncretism to get rid of. Instead, the local culture is an important ingredient in forming the church, its ceremonies and actions. The HKBP has had a tradition of pietism from the very beginning. Today, it is instead the Charismatic movement that is influencing the HKBP, at least to some extent. In an attempt not to lose members to the Charismatic movement, many HKBP parishes are searching for new forms for celebrating its service, preferably by including a second, more open and less formal service on Sundays. In that way the HKBP hopes to be able to

297. Damanik, Janri. Interview.
298. Pardede, Erlina. Interview.
299. Ibid.
300. Nainggolan, Binsar. Interview.

maintain the old tradition as a church at the same time as they can hold on to members by introducing new elements.

4

Living with Contradictions

The descriptions in the previous chapter give interesting and important information about each church, showing, among other things, how they are struggling to give form to their Christian belief in the situation in which each church lives. All of them are confronted by social, political, religious, and historical realities and all of them have to consider many parameters before making a decision or acting in that reality.

FOUR DILEMMAS

The images of the churches in the previous chapter[1] will be analyzed by bringing to light a few dilemmas that seem to occupy the churches, that is, the dilemmas of (1) "community *and* pluralism," (2) "power *and* servanthood," (3) how to be "an alternative to culture *and* be affirmative of culture" and (4) how to handle being both "inward *and* outward."

The chapter is structured by the four dilemmas. A few examples from the churches are mentioned for each dilemma. They are not to be understood as a complete list of what is said about the dilemmas in the empirical material. Rather they are just examples of the dilemmas that feature in the material. As mentioned, any of the five churches could have been chosen to discuss any of the dilemmas but in this chapter two are chosen for each dilemma and their approaches to handling the dilemma are described. A theological discussion of the dilemma is presented in this chapter and is

---

1. In this chapter I will not use footnotes that refer to the empirical material since nothing new is introduced that cannot easily be found in the previous descriptions of the churches.

undertaken in relation to how the dilemma is understood and handled in the church. This is intended to show what turns out to be important for the churches when they are handling the dilemmas. What are they considering or what are they taking into account in doing this? One could say that relating a systematic theological discussion to the dilemmas these churches are handling helps to clarify what it is that is of importance for them. Ultimately, this approach makes it possible to discuss in what ways the churches are using their Lutheran heritage when confronting and handling the dilemmas.

COMMUNITY *AND* PLURALISM

Most communities—societies in general as well as church communities—are made up of people who resemble each other in various ways. This is a well-known phenomenon that has frequently been discussed, not least in political philosophy. How can we as humans live together in peace and harmony if we are different from each other and belong to different religions, political fractions, ethnicities and so on?

Just as difficulties with living together are constantly present in society in general, so are they in the life of churches. In the following I will give examples of how two of the churches in this study try to handle the dilemma of "community *and* pluralism." Note, however, that choosing the IECLB and the FLM for this does not imply that it is only these churches which face this dilemma. As I see it, all five churches are in a similar situation. They all have to handle the dilemma of community and pluralism in one way or another; the ILCO by balancing between being a church solely for the poor and being a church in which different groups feels at home; the ELCI by trying to be a pluralistic and open folk church and at the same time create parish communities for those who seek a true community, communities that some could see as more closed; and the HKBP by finding a way to be church when it is trapped between its vision of being a church with a gospel to present to the whole population and the realities in their country that make the HKBP a "prisoner" in its own domain.

The IECLB, Brazil—Transformation from an Ethnic Church

Ever since its foundation the IECLB has had a German heritage as its core identity. The need to create and uphold a community for German descendants has been both important and expected by many. To some extent the IECLB has served as a shelter for its members in a sometimes hostile environment. But the need for this function is no longer perceived as relevant, either by society in general or by most members of the church. The German-speaking population has become more integrated in Brazilian society than it was just fifty years ago and it is less evident that Lutheran families succeed in passing on their German-Lutheran heritage to the next generation. As a result, when people today describe the IECLB they tend to single out other things than the German language and the German heritage. In short, the IECLB is undergoing a transformation from one type of church to another. The old way of being a church does not function in the new social circumstances. At the same time it cannot be abandoned.

The IECLB sees the transformation from an ethnic to a pluralistic church not just as necessary because times are changing but also as a welcome, theologically relevant development. At the same time, the IECLB perceives a risk of splitting into smaller churches. One way of dealing with this has been to open up for different ways of expressing oneself inside the IECLB, so that the IECLB as a church organization harbors diversity that may differ from parish to parish.

Today, the IECLB practices traditional Lutheran worship as well as more Evangelically inspired forms. Some of its members define themselves as liberation theologians, others have more conservative views. There are city parishes and rural parishes. One could say that in the past the IECLB was a church with great diversity but always within certain ethnic boundaries. Today, the ethnic identity is slowly disappearing and other demarcations seem to be becoming important, such as economic barriers and gender.

The FLM, Madagascar—Finding New Ways to Include Pluralism

The FLM is a huge church and is growing rapidly. Some say that one new congregation is established every week. It is also a church in a very poor country with most of its members in rural areas and poorly educated. Madagascar's Christian history is relatively short; Christianity was even forbidden for over three decades in the nineteenth century. The traditional culture is still strong; almost half of the island's population adheres to the traditional religion. Some say that the religious core of Madagascans, whether or not they are Christian, involves pleasing the spirits. Leaders in the FLM consider that there is—or has been—a tendency for people to adhere to some of the traditional cultural and religious customs at the same time as they attend church and call themselves Christians. Historically, the

FLM has tried to alter or prevent this syncretism, without much success. This desire to keep Christianity free from syncretism has, among other things, led to a rather strict view of what is considered to be Christian or not. One could say that the FLM has resisted some types of pluralism in an attempt to safeguard the Gospel.

How Bonhoeffer Addresses the Dilemma

Dietrich Bonhoeffer addressed the question of community and pluralism, which had engaged him for many years, in what is probably his best-known book, *Life Together*. He wrote it in the course of just four weeks after the Gestapo had closed the theological seminary in Finkenwalde and it represents an attempt to summarize and structure what he had been a part of in recent years. His aim was to reflect—from a pastoral point of view—on what he had written in the 1920s in *Sanctorum Communio*.[2] Developments in the meantime had led him from theoretical to practical thinking. In Finkenwalde he had tried to "live" what he had previously written about. *Life Together* addresses what he considered to be the primary task: preventing the Christian community from becoming a closed community or sect. For Bonhoeffer, a Christian community must always strive to be an open community with room for everyone, not just for those who automatically see one another as friends, equals or likeminded.

These thoughts are expressed concisely in five chapters: "Community," "The Day Together," "The Day Alone," "Service," and "Confession and the Lord's Supper." Having considered aspects of the Christian community in the first four chapters, he finally comes to the Lord's supper.

> The day of the Lord's supper is a joyous occasion for the Christian community. Reconciled in their hearts with God and one another, the community of faith receives the gift of Jesus Christ's body and blood, therein receiving forgiveness, new life, and salvation. New community with God and one another is given to it. The community of the holy Lord's supper is above all fulfillment of the Christian community. Just as the members of the community of faith are united in body and blood at the table of the Lord, so they will be together in eternity. Here the community has reached its goal. Here joy in Christ and Christ's community is complete. The life

2. See for example Green, *Bonhoeffer*.

together of Christians under the word has reached it fulfillment in the sacrament.³

For Bonhoeffer, the Lord's supper is a place of true community, a community with God but also with fellow human beings. It is something you cannot do on your own. You need to be in communion with others and they need to be in communion with you. You need their forgiveness and they need yours, according to Bonhoeffer. The thinking is based on the doctrine of justification, he says, i.e. our righteousness is righteousness from outside (*extra nos*). The Christian is searching for forgiveness by the Word of God and as the Word is put in the mouth of humans, a Christian needs another Christian to give the word of forgiveness.⁴ God's liberating word is given by another person. Bonhoeffer goes on to say that this makes it important that the Christian community is not just a community for the successful or a community when everything is going well, a community that cannot cope with sin. A Christian community's reality is apparent when it confronts real sin. A community that cannot deal with sin, a community that functions only as long as it is a pious community, deprives all its members of help with personal sin. The community must be open and tolerant in how it sees everyone's sins, not just those of some people, according to Bonhoeffer.⁵ Carrying other people's sins involves praying for one another, forgiveness and also speaking the word of God in the form of consolation. You are obliged to let the word of God come forth from your lips, says Bonhoeffer, no matter how hard you find it. As a Christian, you are compelled to touch God and give the Word of God to fellow human beings. However, says Bonhoeffer, the essential foundation for all such meetings is that both parties meet as sinners before God; both are in need of grace.⁶ In that way the community will make room for God's grace and be a true community of persons standing together before God.

This community is feasible, according to Bonhoeffer. Through Christ it is here for everyone to take part in. Christ has made peace between God and humans and also made peace between humans possible. The way to reach a fellow person is no longer blocked by the Self as it was prior to Christ. Communion between people is determined not by ourselves but by what Christ has done for us. I'm someone's brother due to what Christ did

3. Bonhoeffer, *Life Together*, 118.
4. Ibid., 31.
5. Ibid., 108–18.
6. Ibid., 102–7.

for me and vice versa, he says. Through Christ, and only through Christ, can a community of love and service be created.⁷ It cannot be built by human effort; it must be built on Christ.

Bonhoeffer distinguishes between spiritual and emotional love. In the Christian community it is spiritual love that should prevail. Yet, says Bonhoeffer the opposite is often the case. When that happens in a Christian community, the community is transformed from Christ-centeredness to human-centeredness. People in an emotional community let their power over others become visible. The strong may, for example, be admired or feared by the weak.⁸ Spiritual love between people—the foundation of the Christian community—makes a non-consuming community. The other is loved as he or she is, because he or she is already loved by Christ. There shall be no desire to change or master others.⁹ The Christian community cannot be rooted in a desire to have fellowship with just a certain type of people on account of their characteristics or opinions. Its foundation is the fact that its participants are redeemed and called to faith, Bonhoeffer says.¹⁰

> Two factors, which are really one and the same thing, reveal the difference between spiritual and self-centered love. Emotional, self-centered love cannot tolerate the dissolution of a community that has become false, even for the sake of genuine community. And such self-centered love cannot love an enemy, That is to say, one who seriously and stubbornly resists it. Both spring from the same source: the emotional love is by its very nature desire, desire for self-centered community. As long as it can possibly satisfy this desire, it will not give it up, even for the sake of truth, even for the sake of genuine love for others. But the emotional, self-centered love is at an end when it can no longer expect its desire to be fulfilled, namely, in the face of an enemy. There it turns into hatred, contempt, and slander.¹¹

According to Bonhoeffer, spiritual love sees the other as he or she is without trying to change anything. Spiritual love allows the distance that exists between two people to continue to be there because it is Christ who

---

7. Ibid., 32–33.
8. Ibid., 27.
9. Ibid., 43–47.
10. Ibid., 34.
11. Ibid., 43.

stands between them, but in doing so it is also Christ who unites them.[12] Bonhoeffer notes that every human must be understood as a person with whom Christ already has a relationship. It is therefore not permissible to force someone to change into being something that Christ did not do when he received him or her (i.e., you need to see the other person as Christ sees him, without wanting to change anything).[13] Self-centered love constructs its own image of other persons, what they are and what they should become, Bonhoeffer says. It sort of puts the other person's life in my own hands and thereby changes it to my liking. Spiritual love, on the other hand, recognizes the other person's true image as seen from the perspective of Jesus Christ. In that way I see Christ when I meet another person, even if he or she is not like me in any way, Bonhoeffer argues.

This view of spiritual love and the relationship between people leads Bonhoeffer to argue that, to be a true community, the Christian community must not construct itself in such a way that it places people outside it without any possibility of coming in: "... a life together under the Word will stay healthy only when it does not shape itself into a movement, an order, a society, a collegium pietatis."[14] If you are trying to found a community on something that does not give everyone the same opportunities, it will inevitably become a sect.[15]

> The exclusion of the weak and insignificant, the seemingly useless people, from everyday Christian life in community [Lebensgemeinschaft] may actually mean the exclusion of Christ, for in the poor sister or brother, Christ is knocking at the door.[16]

Bonhoeffer also notes that the Christian community must not be driven into a position where the experience of what the community gives back to its participants is what holds it together. Such good experiences may occur and are not negative, but they are coincidences given by grace and should not be what shapes and sustains community,[17] "We are bound together by faith, not by experience."[18] Here lies a great danger to the Christian community, according to Bonhoeffer. The existing Community in a

12. Ibid., 44.
13. Ibid.
14. Ibid., 45.
15. Ibid.
16. Ibid., 45–46.
17. Ibid., 47.
18. Ibid.

church may easily seem not to meet certain people's requirements; criticism can come from both priests and parishioners.[19] But then, Bonhoeffer says, you do not understand that the Community is a gift of God and nothing a person can ask for. It is a spiritual reality. Only God knows the status of the Community. He writes, "The Christian community is not an ideal we have to realize, but rather a reality created by God in Christ in which we may participate."[20] Even the difficulties that arise between people in a community point to God. When you see other people's shortcomings in the community, you should realize that they cannot manage without God's grace and in that case it also applies to me, he says. You cannot trust in yourself or your deeds. We are all under God's judgment and forgiveness and so we belong together.[21]

> This dismisses at the outset every unhappy desire for something more. Those who want more than what Christ has established between us do not want Christian community. They are looking for some extraordinary experiences of community that were denied them elsewhere. Such people are bringing confused and tainted desires into the Christian community. Precisely at this point Christian community is most often threatened from the very outset by the greatest danger, the danger of internal poisoning, the danger of confusing Christian community with some wishful image of pious community, the danger of blending the devout heart's natural desire for community with the spiritual reality of Christian community.[22]

Striving to establish a spiritual community includes trying to serve each other. Bonhoeffer mentions three ways in which this can be manifested: listening, helping and carrying one another's burdens. Listening means active listening, including a willingness to understand the other person and let him or her be heard as he or she wants to be understood. Helping is about seeing where my help is needed and ceasing to do what I'm doing as soon as I understand someone needs me, even if what I am doing is important. I need to help the person God has put in front of me, without coming with excuses, Bonhoeffer says.[23] As to carrying one another's burdens, Bonhoeffer says that the natural reaction when faced with someone else's burden is

19. Ibid., 37–38.
20. Ibid., 38.
21. Ibid., 36–37.
22. Ibid., 34–35.
23. Ibid., 98–107.

to look in another direction. That is not an option for a Christian. He must live in equanimity with his brother and take care of him.[24] Bonhoeffer puts it, "[o]nly as a burden is the other really a brother or sister and not just an object to be controlled."[25] Furthermore, he writes:

> First of all, it is the freedom of the other, mentioned earlier, that is a burden to Christians. The freedom of the other goes against Christians' high opinions of themselves, and yet they must recognize it. Christians could rid themselves of this burden by not giving other persons their freedom, thus doing violence to the personhood of others and stamping their own image on others. But when Christians allow God to create God's own image in others, they allow others their freedom. Thereby Christians themselves bear the burden of the freedom enjoyed by these other creatures of God. All that we mean by human nature, individuality, and talent is part of the other person's freedom—as are the other's weaknesses and peculiarities that so sorely try our patience, and everything that produces the plethora of clashes, differences, and arguments between me and the other. Here, bearing the burden of the other means tolerating the reality of the other's creation by God—affirming it, and in bearing with it, breaking through to delight in it.[26]

A real challenge to the act of service to one another is, according to Bonhoeffer, expressed in Luke 9:46, "An argument arose among them as to which one of them was the greatest." For Bonhoeffer, this sentence is central to an understanding of the processes in a community. It is natural but equally dangerous for the community's survival. For Bonhoeffer, this comparison with others is simply a way of justifying oneself by judging others. But, Bonhoeffer asks, seen from the perspective of Christ, are not the pious as good as the not so pious, are not the talented and the untalented entitled to the same position in the community, and who can claim that the incompetent are not the most pious?[27] For this behavior, Bonhoeffer says, only the Spirit of grace can really help, but the individual must strive for it by refusing to use words or thoughts of judgment of others.

> They can now allow other Christians to live freely, just as God has brought them face to face with each other. The view of such

24. Ibid., 100.
25. Ibid.
26. Ibid., 101.
27. Ibid., 93–94.

> persons expands and, thru their amazement, they recognize for the first time the richness of God's creative glory shining over their brothers and sisters. God did not make others as I would have made them. God did not give them to me so that I could dominate and control them. Now other people, in the freedom with which they were created, become an occasion for me to rejoice, whereas before they were only a nuisance and trouble for me. God does not want me to mold others into the image that seems good to me, that is, into my own image. Instead, in their freedom from me God made other people in God's own image.[28]

In this way, the differences within the community cease to be a source of difficulty; they are transformed instead into joy and gratitude for diversity, according to Bonhoeffer.[29] It will lead to a desire to place oneself, not on top of, but rather among, "... the wretched and lowly."[30] There the other's will, and the other's honor will be accentuated at the expense of my own desire to fame.[31]

For Bonhoeffer, the Christian community goes hand in hand with openness. The community is necessary for the Christian person. In it we meet God, the Word of God and God's grace and forgiveness; in that way the community gives strength to the participant to live his or her life outside the community. But when Bonhoeffer writes of community, he never means a closed community, it is always an open community that has room for different answers to God's call.

The Situation in the IECLB Seen in Relation to Bonhoeffer

What Bonhoeffer discusses is not just a theological problem, but a real dilemma for most churches. The IECLB is one of them. The way in which the IECLB handles this dilemma in practice differs from parish to parish. In some parishes, the different "traditions" or views about worship and theology come together in practical church life and thereby learn from each other. In others, the different groups or positions formally belong together but seldom meet. An example is the celebration of Sunday worship. In some cases the parishioners either attend both the traditional and a Charismatic service or alternate between the types of service. In other cases it is more

---

28. Ibid., 95.
29. Ibid.
30. Ibid., 96.
31. Ibid., 96–97.

a matter of two different congregations that never meet even though they belong to the same community.

The IECLB's history, organization and structure make it a large and important church for society in general as well as for many individuals. But the same history, organization and structure also limit the possibilities of choosing the road ahead. All these factors entail major responsibilities for the IECLB in relation to people, society and history that it has to consider in everything it does. If relevant aspects are dropped too readily, people who feel at home in the IECLB today and may have done so for generations will be liable to feel estranged. At the same time, if the IECLB were to stick to its old, narrower identity, in the long run it may lose numerous members. So the IECLB tries to find a solution that combines the different forms of community and pluralism. As we have seen earlier, researcher Wilhelm Wachholz describes the situation by saying that the IECLB lives with a constant tension. One could say that to some extent, in order to handle what is happening the IECLB wants to function as a frame around radically different views of the church.

But what would happen in the IECLB if the church were to say "no" to acting as a frame for pluralism and aimed instead at promoting real pluralism, in the sense Bonhoeffer discusses? That is, a pluralism whereby people really meet, learn from each other and have ethical demands on each other, even if all they have in common is their belief in God.

According to Bonhoeffer, every church, in whatever situation, must never stop reflecting on how to create a community built on pluralism. Christ has opened the way for that and with His help we as persons and as churches can achieve a great deal, even though we cannot attain the goal. Christian community goes hand in hand with openness. Community is necessary for a Christian person. In it we meet God, the Word of God and God's grace and forgiveness. In that way the community gives the participant strength to live his or her life outside the community. But when Bonhoeffer writes of community, he never means a closed community, always an open community that has room for different answers to God's call.

The way in which the IECLB handles a pluralistic situation is not confined to this church. It is to be found in whole church families as well as in local congregations.[32] It could be a fruitful way of dealing with a complicated or problematic situation, depending on how this is seen and done. It can be said that providing room for different views of theology or different

---

32. See for example Blåder, *Gemenskap och mångfald*.

ways of acting in the church is not sufficient if they never meet. If they simply function like islands, unconnected by bridges. Pluralism as such is not enough, it must be a pluralism whereby "others" confront or meet each other. It is in this otherness that we meet Christ. The challenge is to create a milieu that, besides being open for everyone—functioning as a frame for otherness—enables real encounters that include active service for each other. A milieu that functions not just as an umbrella under which people work or live alone, but one that creates as many opportunities as possible for meeting the other, hearing the other's ethical demands and letting others hear my ethical demands on them.

The understanding of community *and* pluralism in the IECLB could be seen as understandable, but also problematic. They see and want to embrace pluralism but to what extent are they trying to create a community with diversity, not just isolated islands? On the other hand, if the IECLB had handled the situation in such a way that people felt that pluralism forces them to have real encounters, the outcome would possibly have been more complicated, with probably less people feeling at home in the church.

When dealing with the dilemma of community *and* pluralism, the IECLB finds it most important to do this in such a way that the church is understood and seen as open for others besides German descendants. This, combined with outside pressure from Charismatic movements and various interests inside the IECLB, leads the church to see the importance of making room for diversity. Milieus need to be created in which people feel at home, so the church does not lose members and attracts new members. So for handling the dilemma, community becomes important, just like pluralism, while achieving a combination seems harder.

The Situation in the FLM Seen in Relation to Bonhoeffer

According to Bonhoeffer, a church should strive to be a community filled with diversity instead of for the like-minded. A Christian community cannot be an entirely homogeneous organization. First, that would not be possible since all communities are made up of people and people differ, (i.e., it would necessitate an infinite range of boundaries). Second, because a church should be a community of people who are redeemed and called by God, not of those who think or act alike. It should be a community in which no one should need to change in order to be a member; you can belong as you are. If God, by calling, has already said yes to a person, members of the community have no right to try to turn that person into someone else. The

Church must be understood as a community based on the will of Christ, not on the will of persons. It is therefore a community whose members should act in favor of each other. The Church should be a community of people who in faith bear one another's burdens, not a community of people who "match" each other. It is God's love that holds the community together, not people's opinions about each other.

Seen in this way, community and pluralism is not something a church can either have or do without. It must be something every Christian community needs to seek and try to establish. At the same time, it is an ideal that cannot be achieved, at least in full. But churches still have to aim for it. A Christian church must hope and look for ways of establishing a good relation between community and pluralism.

Following Bonheoffer's line of thought, there are many reasons for striving so that community and pluralism can go hand in hand to create a community full of diversity, a community with no strict boundaries between "in" and "out," right and wrong. However, the FLM also has many—and good—reasons for acting as it does, being strict in relation to syncretism. Its decisions are informed by its history and social situation with a rapidly expanding church, a desire not to be directed by the values of churches in the "north," its situation in a country with a lively traditional culture and religion; and many other factors. The remedy—be stricter about syncretism—is understandable but also problematic. Understandable in terms of the FLM's history and social reality, problematic in relation to a theology of sociality as Bonheoffer's.

In handling the dilemma of community and pluralism in the church's practical life, it seems to be clear that the FLM is greatly affected by the strength of the traditional culture, not least as regards the belief in spirits. Ever since it was founded, the FLM has therefore struggled with a great deal of syncretism. This circumstance and the importance—seen from the FLM's viewpoint—of a clear "yes" to Jesus from every individual in order to build the kingdom of God and the importance of the church helping so that they are able to say that "yes," seem to be the main factors in the FLM's ways of handling the dilemma.

The situation for the FLM is evident and their reaction to syncretism is understandable but seen in relation to Bonheoffer's thoughts about sociality, it can be problematized. Christian history is full of attempts to defend the church from heresies and those who have been perceived as heretics have mostly had to leave the church. However, many theologians—of whom

Bonhoeffer is one—would say that such a classification is problematic. It is important to be aware that no one can be certain about who is "in" or who is "out." That is not a matter for humans to decide. We are not in a position to make correct judgments about other people. Only God can do that and we must therefore leave it to God. Another point is that no one can ever be free of sin; we can fight against sin in various ways but can never be free of it. As we all live in an imperfect world, it can be said that besides being something we as humans cannot free ourselves from, sin functions as a sign of God to others. A person facing another person's sin ought to conclude that, just as that person is a sinner, so am I and therefore we are both in need of forgiveness. In that way, other people's sin draws us to God by giving us a perspective on our own relation with God. In the long run this also means that other sinners must be able to be part of the community, just as I as a sinner would like to be a part. As we have seen, Bonhoeffer expressed this by talking about spiritual and emotional love. In a Christian community it is the spiritual love that should prevail but, as Bonhoeffer notes, the opposite is often the case. When that happens, the community undergoes a transformation from Christ-centeredness to human-centeredness. In the emotional community, people manifest their power over others. The strong may, for example, derive admiration or fear from the weak.[33] Spiritual love between people, which is the foundation of the Christian community, does not work like that: the other is loved as he or she is, because he or she is already loved by Christ. There shall be no desire to change or master others.[34] The Christian community cannot be rooted in a desire to have fellowship with only a certain type of people on account of their characteristics or opinions. The only basis for a Christian community is that the participants are redeemed and called to faith.[35]

In relation to the dilemma of community and pluralism, it is interesting to see how the Fifohazana movement has been growing, due in part to cultural recognition, in part to support from the FLM. In the Fifohazana, people found a God who was stronger than the spirits, which was important for getting people to choose and adhere to Christianity without mixing it with traditional beliefs. One could say that the Fifohazana highlights a theme in Christianity that is clearly intelligible in terms of the traditional culture. In that way the FLM is using traditional culture so that Christianity

33. Bonhoeffer, *Life Together*, 27.
34. Ibid., 43–47.
35. Ibid., 34.

can be understood in a good or proper way and thereby point to a road that leads to Christ. But it could also be said that the FLM tries to handle this situation by opening up for understandings of the Christian belief that in some way could incorporate features of the traditional belief, and in that way make new room for pluralism in the community.

POWER *AND* SERVANTHOOD

History is full of positive uses of power, but also of abuses. Similarly, it is full of good servanthood and misuse of servanthood. And just as all this is to be found in secular society, so it can be found in Christian history at large. Whether one admits it or not, power has a relation to theology, churches and Christian praxis. Different approaches to power are to be seen even in the Bible and both positive and negative approaches to power are accordingly to be found in Christian history. Even today, every church has to constantly problematize and discuss the relation between power and servanthood in one way or another. Even if they exist in different circumstances and contexts, the dilemma is the same.

The following examples refer to the ELCI and the ILCO. But just as with the dilemma of community *and* pluralism, the dilemma of power *and* servanthood is discernable in all five churches: in the IECLB when it is discussing organizational forms in a changing society and a changing religious milieu; in the HKBP in the attempt to steer clear of controversies with the Muslim majority society; and in the FLM not least in the relation between the church and the regime.

The ELCI, Iceland—Bringing a Powerful History

Being a church connected with the state makes the ELCI in Iceland different in many ways from the other churches in this study. Throughout the ELCI's history, church and state have empowered one another. This historic relation has to some extent resulted in a very powerful church. The church has given the state divine sanction and the state has used its secular power to support the church when needed. Today the situation is different but church and state still give each other some form of legitimacy.

This special status confers opportunities and privileges that are not available to any other church or religious institution. It "opens doors" to society for the ELCI in a special way, to institutions as well as to people. Moreover, the power from the relation to the state gives the ELCI a strong voice in society and public debate and, not least, a very strong financial base that enables the ELCI to be present throughout Iceland. At the same time the ELCI wants to be seen as a servant church in terms of being an open folk church empowering, not itself but people in church and society.

This relation to the state and the power it brings are now being questioned more and more frequently, even from inside the church. Icelandic society is changing rapidly from a homogenous to a pluralistic, multi-religious society and this has altered the role of the ELCI. It is by far the largest religious organization in Iceland but not the only one, and more and more people, both outside and inside the church, are seeing the problems or questions that have to be solved with a powerful church in a pluralistic society.

The ILCO, Costa Rica—Empowering the Powerless

Whereas the ELCI in Iceland, through its history and connection to the state, is a powerful church, the ILCO in Costa Rica is its opposite: young, very small and living, one could say, on the periphery of society. This society is hierarchical and the ILCO wants to understand itself as something different, something that serves, rather than being served; it wants to empower, rather than having power. While it is small and peripheral—and in that way powerless—it has acquired power by being a distinct voice from below in controversial social issues. So although it lacks formal power, it is not powerless. It obtains power by giving voice to those below, from the poor and marginalized groups that do not normally have a voice.

The whole enterprise would probably have been impossible, or at least hard to implement, if the ILCO's attitude had been to see power as something a church should not possess. At the same time, as we know, having power can corrupt. For the ILCO, some form of power is needed to gain access to the public debate and be heard and taken seriously; but this entails a risk that, in time, the same power will transform the ILCO into something it does not want to be, a powerful institution.

How Sykes Addresses the Dilemma

In his book *Power and Christian Theology*, Stephen Sykes addresses the time-honored question of power and relates it to Christian theology and the church. Sykes writes from a perspective that includes his own experiences as an academic professor and a bishop in the Anglican Church. His starting point is Robert Kagan's essay *Paradise and Power: America and Europe in the New world order*, in which Kagan—according to Sykes—argues that the willingness to see and use power as a means depends on the actual power one possesses. Kagan quotes a saying "When you have a hammer, all problems look like nails" but adds that when you don't have a hammer, you don't want anything to look like a nail.[36] For Sykes this raises the question of whether it is the European churches' relatively weak status today that lies behind their very reluctant attitude to power? The history of the Christian church is indicative. In times of strength, churches' attitude to power has seldom been negative.

> . . . can one trace a similar history of correlation in the case of theology, to that to which Kagan points in the case of politics? Was a strong and influential Church, deeply entwined with structure of government, inclined to look positively at the phenomenon of power, whereas a week, marginalized Church has had all manner of anxieties and reservations about the same subject?[37]

Two of the seven chapters in Sykes' book present examples of and discuss what for him are the two main approaches to power in Christian theology: affirmation and rejection of power, respectively. In other chapters he discusses the power of the church in public life and the power inside the church. It is of course a simplification to say that there are two ways of relating to power in the Christian church, one positive, the other negative; the question is much more complicated and could be analyzed accordingly. However, these opposite trends are sufficient for his purpose and show that there are very different approaches to power.[38]

The affirmation of human power has two manifestations in Christian theology. The first views the church as an agent in a cosmic drama where the church's power is linked to the power of God. That justified the church as a bearer of power. The second affirms civil power, that is, civil authorities are understood as deriving their power from God.[39] These two approaches are often intertwined and sometimes seen separately. Evidence of this tradition of approving of power in different forms is found by Sykes in the early church. Not that power has been affirmed in some periods of history and rejected in others. Rather, that the two approaches to power have lived side

---

36. Sykes, *Power and Christian Theology*, ix.
37. Ibid., ix–x.
38. Ibid., 28.
39. Ibid., 27.

by side throughout history. However, when it comes to the affirmation of power, Sykes mentions what Paul writes in the Letter to the Romans: "there is no authority except from God, and those authorities that exist have been instituted by God" (Rom 13:1).[40] According to Sykes, this verse, among many others, has been used for the affirmation of different forms of power. He discusses the eschatological thinking in the early church and argues that it had an impact on how to relate to power. At a time when people were sure of the Son of God's imminent return, what mattered was not to organize the church or possess power but to live a good and holy life, which seldom included striving for power.[41]

> Plainly there is a difference between a community whose conduct is partly determined by the brief interval before the end, and a community that is forcefully instructed not to be impressed with any suggestion of its imminence. In the latter much more attention will be given to the existing conditions of society.[42]

According to Sykes, after some time in the young church it was the latter that happened. Besides managing to grow, the church underwent a mental shift. Contrary to expectations, God had not yet returned and there was now a need to show that the power of God was nonetheless with the church even in times of waiting. That need led to God's power being incorporated in the mass, into bread and wine. God was there.[43] The early church started to understand itself in a new way. The relation to the Old Testament was seen in a different light; the church was something new, separate from what had been. The church had a new covenant and a new king—just not yet visible. Sykes points out that interpretations of the old texts began to change; they now underscored the church's new role and the power of Christ. Verses that had previously been interpreted as referring to Israel were now interpreted as referring to Christ. The power that was in the hands of Christ was also seen as being in the hands of the church. Against this background, power and church started to walk side by side, albeit not all the time.

Taking some examples from church history, Sykes then discusses the ambiguous but positive view of power in the church. Eusebius of Caesarea, Augustine and John Calvin exemplify different standpoints and arguments

40. Ibid.
41. Ibid., 29.
42. Ibid.
43. Ibid.

about power but what they have in common is an affirmation of power as a way of demonstrating a favorable relation to God. That goes for the church as well as for individuals. The basis for the affirmation of power is found by Sykes in a selection of bible verses, for instance the above-mentioned Rom 13:1–2.

> Here it may appear to commend passivity, on the one hand; alternatively on the other, it lends itself to deployment in commendation of theocratic government. In terms of the map of the previous chapter, Romans 13 seems to be an example of the triumph of law over anarchy, the implication of divine creation in the theatre of human society. Good government involves the operation of the power of God; "it is God's servant for your good" and "it is the servant of God to execute wrath on the wrong doer" (Rom 13:3 f.) A Christian ruler has a double opportunity of participating in divine sovereignty, first by personally acknowledging the kingdom of God, and secondly by enacting good laws and ruling with justice.[44]

Throughout history, this type of interpretation of scripture has opened up for various approaches to power. Origen, for example, saw God's work in what the emperor Augustus did and Tertulian asked Christians to pray for their emperor; and not only that, he also asked them to pray that the Parousia would be delayed. The world was good as it was.[45] Eusebius of Caesarea celebrated the emperor Constantine with these words: "Thus outfitted in the likeness of the Kingdom of heaven, he pilots affairs below with an upward gaze, to steer by the archetypal form. He grows strong in his model of monarchic rule, which the Ruler of All has given to the race of men alone of those on earth."[46] In short, having power has been understood as being standing under God's grace and so it was a Christian duty to honor the emperor. Discussing Augustine, Sykes finds his arguments more nuanced than those of many others, not least in *The City of God*.[47] Augustine is affirmative of power but sees problems and difficulties. For Sykes, when Augustine writes about power, he is both cautious and sophisticated. "The result in *The City of God* is certainly no synthesis; but set in the dramatic context of a cosmic struggle between hosts of angels and demons the issues are given

---

44. Ibid., 48.
45. Ibid., 33.
46. Ibid., 32. Sykes is quoting *Laus Constantini* from the year 335–336 by Eusebios of Caesarea.
47. Ibid., 49–53.

a rare depth. The response to power is fundamentally affirming, but there are more than hints of reservation."[48] Sykes also notes that Augustine paved the way for thoughts about the relation between church and emperor that were to have a major impact in the Middle Ages.[49]

As said, according to Sykes, there are certain opinions in church history that reject power more profoundly. Here, too, the foundation lies in different approaches to power that are to be found in the Bible. Sykes stresses that the approach to power is, of course, not homogeneous, but rather something that stems from "the realization that power presents a problem."[50] An example is, according to Sykes, Mark 10:42–45.

> So, Jesus called them and said to them, "You know that among the Gentiles those whom they recognize as their rulers lord it over them, and their great ones are tyrants over them. But it is not so among you; but whoever wishes to become great among you must be your servant, and whoever wishes to be first among you must be slave of all. For the Son of Man came not to be served but to serve, and to give his life a ransom for many."[51]

This exemplifies the radical difference between Christian and gentile approaches to power. Here the Christian relation is modeled on being the servant of others, which means that one cannot become great, at least not by wielding power. To build his case, Sykes cites some theologians from church history. One of them is Marsilius (1275–1342), who in *The Defender of Peace* discusses power within the church. He claims that all power belongs to Christ, who will use it; but that is not for us to see today, we must wait for the Parousia, when this will happen. Today, disciples of Christ can do nothing but warn, the church can do nothing else; all action must come from civil authorities, not from the church. Things will change and the roles will be reversed but until then the church must live powerless.[52] Sykes also mentions Luther as a source that has been used for the rejection of power, not least Luther's reaction to the Peasants' War and his doctrine of the two kingdoms, which had a tremendous effect among churches and societies in Lutheran areas. A modern German theologian whom Sykes uses as an example of a theologian rejecting power is Jürgen Moltmann.

48. Ibid., 53.
49. Ibid., 35.
50. Ibid., 57.
51. Ibid., 55.
52. Ibid., 60–61.

To elicit Moltmann's view on power, Sykes turns to the final chapter of *The Trinity and the Kingdom of God*, where Moltmann makes what for him is an important distinction between monotheism and Trinity; he writes, "The notion of a divine monarchy in heaven and on earth . . . generally provides the justification for earthly domination—religious, moral, patriarchal or political domination—and makes it a hierarchy, a 'holy rule.'"[53] Here Moltmann finds reasons or grounds for political power, which he calls "political monotheism," as well as for church power, which he calls "clerical monotheism." For Moltmann, both are in opposition to the genuine doctrine of the Trinity, which is what the church should strive for.[54] Monotheism leads to hierarchy, power and submission, whereas the Trinity is built on true brotherhood or sisterhood, on equality, which is what the true church should aim for. Moltmann also discusses the three kingdoms that could be seen and that manifest themselves at different times in history. They could be understood as different stages; first there is the kingdom of the Father, the creator, then the kingdom of the Son, the redeemer, and finally the kingdom of the Spirit, in which no one is above anyone else. We are all equal and all friends of God.[55]

By refining two views of power in the history of the church, the affirmative and the negatory, Sykes shows that there have been and are different views on power in Christian theology and this has been handled in different ways. He also shows that these two approaches to power have legitimate reasons. Both are to be found in the Old as well as the New Testament. And both have featured and been used in church history. So where does this take us? First it must be said that for Sykes the conclusion is neither affirmation nor rejection of power in any simple form. Instead of being a problem that can be solved once and for all by choosing the right path, he is clear that power is something which has to be seen, understood and handled continuously. It is a dilemma.

For Sykes, the road to an understanding of a Christian response to power lies in the sacrifice of Christ. Everything ends in fulfillment and in the rule of God. This is important for Sykes but at the same time the death of Christ "addresses the individual oppression, corporate manipulation and cosmic disorder which is the human situation."[56] All life finds itself in a

---

53. Ibid., 74. Sykes is quoting Moltmann, *Trinity and the Kingdom of God*.
54. Ibid., 74.
55. Ibid., 76.
56. Ibid., 152.

situation where different powers are at work, overlapping each other. We are not and cannot live in a power-free zone. According to Sykes, we are then liable to be so confused that we do not act at all, which for him is not an adequate way of dealing with power.[57] Instead it is the focus of everything on the cross, the creation, redemption, and eschatology that opens up for an understanding of power. The light of the cross makes visible every kind of power, struggling in different directions. Moreover, the cross expresses the future and provides a model for Christian power. However, according to Sykes, although the cross serves as an example, church history shows that this has been abused many, many times. We live in a time of powers and must therefore share a constant ambivalence to power.

> It will be argued, first, that there is an explicit acknowledgement of the plurality of powers in Christian theology, unified in the narrative or drama of creation, redemption and last things, whose central, pivotal event is the crucifixion. Sacrifice, especially the sacrifice of Christ, is about these powers and their relationship. They cease to be a random network in which human beings happen to be trapped at any time, both prisoners and jailers. As these powers are oriented around and interpreted by the death and resurrection of Christ, their potential for good emerges, while (at least in the present life) their ambivalence never entirely vanishes.[58]

Power, for Sykes, will always be a part of this world, regardless of whether or not we see it. There will be power in society, power in church and power in the hands of the individual. We are living in a very complex world and the best way to avoid the dangerous aspects of power is not to ignore it, but to address it, see it and work with it.

The Situation in the ELCI Seen in Relation to Sykes

A brief presentation of the ELCI can easily see it as a powerful church, in the meaning Sykes discusses. The ELCI is an old Lutheran church and for five centuries it has been *the* church in Iceland. As a folk church the ELCI covers the whole of Iceland and meets most of its population in various situations, such as baptisms, weddings and funerals. With such a large proportion of the population as members for so many centuries on an isolated island, the ELCI plays a special role. One could say that it was *the* church in Iceland until quite recently. If you lived in Iceland you were also a member of the

---

57. Ibid., 136.
58. Ibid., 116.

ELCI. The ELCI has funds, buildings, a structure and an organization that no other religious organization in Iceland has. Moreover, it has the trust of Icelanders, generated by centuries of a close relation between church and people. From the outside it is not far-fetched to see all of this—the relation to the state, the many historic church buildings in the country, the large number of employed clergy, the widespread church-related work and the role of the church in civil society—as pointing to the ELCI as a church that could be understood in terms of affirming power, in relation to the examples Sykes presents.

A closer look could reveal a different story, one that rather sets the ELCI in relation to what Sykes would call a church that rejects power, or maybe, more correctly, uses its power to empower both individuals and institutions and in that way puts servanthood first. An important factor here is that the ELCI understands itself as a folk church. Hard as it is to define, the folk church tradition in the ELCI has played an important role in making it an open church with a special emphasis on everyone, not just those who take part in church activities or worship. This openness is probably also what most members of the ELCI associate with their church. It should be a church with few or no specific demands on its members, but open for everyone. The ELCI understands its assignment to be the whole country and everyone, not just the core community. Moreover, the ELCI understands itself as an actor, working together with other actors in society on questions to do with society and people's lives.

By refining two views of power in the history of the church, the affirmative and the rejecting, Stephen Sykes shows that there have been and still are different views of power in Christian theology and that power has been treated in different ways. Sykes concludes that the solution is neither to affirm nor reject power in any simple way. Instead of being a problem that can be solved once and for all by choosing the right path, he is clear that power is something that must be seen, understood and handled continually. It is a dilemma. And this is what the ELCI—like many other churches—is struggling with. It wants to keep its structure and organization, its buildings and churches given by history. In short it wants to keep its power. But at the same time the ELCI understands that nowadays there are problems with bringing a powerful history into new circumstances when society is changing, when people are leaving the church—if not always by withdrawing their membership, but by losing interest—when new churches are emerging and secularization is growing. The ELCI is looking for a way to combine the rejection of power with the affirmation of power in a new setting.

The most important factor in dealing with this dilemma is the church's democratic structure. This organizational structure gives every member of the ELCI the possibility of influencing its future. This is also a way of guaranteeing that power is spread instead of being in the hands of a few professional theologians or priests. It is probably true to say that the ELCI is trying to solve the dilemma of power and servanthood by having a close relation to the state, a majority of the Icelandic people as members and a democratic structure. If the ELCI succeeds in this, one could say that that church and culture are not antagonists, but are integrated into each other, that power is spread throughout the country and to most of the population. In that way power is not a goal, but a means of accomplishing something else—servanthood.

Examples of this will to empower others are the strong social focus, the endeavor to strike a balance between the inner group and responsibility for the whole of society and, not least, the aim of being a free, critical voice in Icelandic society. A recent example of this is the reaction of many people in the ELCI, including many priests, to Iceland's severe economic crisis a few years back, in which the ELCI was a strong voice.

The ELCI is handling the dilemma of power *and* servanthood primarily by trying to uphold the identity of a folk church, with its broad, open approach. In that way it can continue to be a majority church in Iceland, have a good, prosperous relation with the state, and have buildings and employees, as long as the goal is something other than gaining power for its own sake instead of having it in order to be a better servant. The ELCI seems to have an affirmative approach to power, but not primarily as a way of enhancing its status and that of its pastors and leaders, but mainly in order to be able to reach out over Iceland with the gospel. This is also how most of the ELCI's members—active and passive—have wanted it to work. To do that, the ELCI has needed a certain amount of power.

In many ways this means that the ELCI draws conclusions similar to Sykes'. Power will always be present in this world, whether or not we see it. There will be power in society, power in a church and power in the hands of the individual. The world we live in is very complex and the best way to avoid power's dangerous aspects is not to disregard it, but to address it, see it and constantly work on it. The ELCI sees the usefulness of power as a means of accomplishing what they hope to accomplish. Power is not just important, it is a necessity. It is a means for accomplishing what the gospel wants them to accomplish. From that perspective, the goal is not power, but servanthood through power.

The Situation in the ILCO Seen in Relation to Sykes

The ILCO's main goal is not to gain or increase power just for the sake of having it, but to liberate people to a better life and be a servant to those who need it. Being a very small church with progressive ideas in a conservative and traditional culture, this could easily be seen as an impossible task. But as shown, the ILCO's impact on Costa Rican society is far greater than its small membership suggests.

What are often seen as signs of power—money, hierarchy, numerous followers, solid views on ethics, teaching and so on—are not what come to mind when one thinks of the ILCO. Instead, one sees a church that seems to have turned its back on the attributes of power. But while the ILCO is a powerless church in many respects, it does have a great deal of power by being a sign of something else—a counter-image.

There are similarities between the ILCO and how Sykes describes power when relating it to the sacrifice of Christ. The ILCO's work for empowering people who have little or no power in the traditional society makes things happen in society and with people. The traditional order is turned into disorder, the traditional ethical norms are loosened and some sort of uncertainty may arise in society. Just as Sykes reflects about Christ, by doing this the ILCO paves the way for a transformation of society, which means that a different type of power will emerge. As time passes, what has been seen as something powerless—the sacrifice of Christ or the small, insignificant church—is transformed into something powerful.

For Sykes the sacrifice of Christ shows the true face of power. Power is not one-sided or simple to understand and handle. An event can often contain power in both a positive and a negative way simultaneously. It can be used for a future good, but also for domination and conquest. Moreover power can be mistaken for powerlessness and powerlessness can be mistaken for power. In the sacrifice of Christ, the diversified forms of power come together. Things are not what they seem to be and an unforeseen power can arise out of what appeared to be powerless.

What the ILCO is doing could be interpreted along these lines. They are questioning the status quo of power in society, but instead of trying to obtain power for the church institution and thereby change society, they hope and try to turn their powerlessness into something more transformative, a power to come. As Christ turned powerlessness into power, so the ILCO wants to change society from bottom to top by giving people tools to transform society. They do this by seeing people, including those whom others never see, by promoting the self-esteem of those whom society in general would never give a thought, and by giving hope to those whose lives are hopeless. In this way the ILCO uses its powerlessness in a way modeled by Christ.

But this also prompts a question or a reflection. One huge difference between the ILCO and the other churches in this study is its small size. Another is the ILCO's view of itself as a movement. A third is its youth. All organizations need a structure and to maintain that structure power is needed. That is not necessarily a bad thing but in time the structure may grow and become something that is important in itself. The ILCO is not there yet, which makes it easier for them than it probably is for the other churches in this study to act more freely. They have fewer responsibilities to society, their members, and history. But what will the future bring? Will the ILCO be able to go on striving for transformation through powerlessness or will other things become more important for it?

At present, however, one could say that the ILCO is a powerless church in terms of what is normally meant by having power, but a very powerful church when it comes to making an impact on people and society.

ALTERNATIVE TO CULTURE *AND* AFFIRMATIVE OF CULTURE

Defining "culture" is not easy, though many attempts have been made.[59] It is easier to say that by all the usual definitions, all churches have to live within a culture in some form. No individual or church can do otherwise. We use culture when we act. We cannot even speak about God without doing so inside a frame of culture that lays down what is possible to think, say and do. But while some churches affirm culture, saying that as a church it is important to embrace and live in the culture or that they have to live in a culture because they can never escape its grip, there is also an important trend in Christian thinking which claims that Christianity should reject culture. Christianity should be something else. It should represent an alternative to the surrounding culture.

---

59. For a short introduction see for example: Long, *Theology and Culture*.

The dilemma of rejection and affirmation of culture is also to be seen in all the five churches. In the ILCO when the church has to strike a balance between, or chose between, being understood as a relevant voice by most Costa Ricans and being a distinct, critical voice, seen as relevant by just a few; in the ELCI in how it tries to relate to Icelandic society by having a folk church identity and at the same time wants to be a free actor with a free voice that could transform people and society; and the FLM handles the dilemma of wanting to be an alternative culture but at the same time has to cope with a situation where the traditional culture has been strong even inside the church. The other two churches, the HKBP and the IECLB, will be used as examples for the dilemma of affirmation of culture and rejection of culture.

The HKBP, Indonesia—A Chosen and a Forced Culture

In a broad sense the HKBP relates to culture in three distinct ways: in relation to the Muslim majority society, in relation to the different ethnic cultures in Indonesia, and in relation to a Christian culture that is changing. The present politically tense situation more or less forces the HKBP to refrain from engaging in the political and social debates in Indonesian society. It has to be very careful in everything it does not to exacerbate existing tensions. This situation is reinforcing a tendency right from the start for the HKBP to stay within its boundaries and not engage in larger cultural discussions with the majority society. Another topic for discussion in the HKBP is the ethnic Batak culture. Syncretism has always been present in the church. People have used Christian rites and thoughts along with traditional Batak rites and thoughts. The solution, ever since Nommensen's day, has been, not to avoid or exclude the traditional culture, but to "Christianize" it. This is still often the case. Traditional Batak culture, with its rites and symbols, continues to be there but with a Christian meaning or interpretation. But as we have seen, this is not always the case; some traditional cultural phenomena are not changing or doing so very slowly, not least the role of women in society. The HKBP also faces changes in Christian culture. The expansive Charismatic movement is introducing new ways of living the Christian life and new forms of worship. This is not being handled by trying to totally avoid these influences, partly because that might risk losing members and partly because some of the pastors are interested in what the Charismatic movement has to offer the HKBP. The relation between church and culture is complicated in the HKBP, founded as it is in its history and largely under pressure from external factors. As a result, decisions about church and culture often have to allow for what is happening elsewhere.

The IECLB, Brazil—An Including Way

The situation for the IECLB in Brazil today could probably be characterized by stating that the historically close relation between church and culture in the IECLB has changed into different relations that point in a multitude of directions. The close relation between the church and the German culture is still there and is understood as important, but other parts of the church are moving in other directions. One tendency is to strive for a better society and better living conditions for the marginalized and poor. Another is more charismatic, building parishes with a stronger sense of community and with a type of theology that differs from what has normally been the case. The IECLB houses different understandings of what a church should be and do and it therefore also houses different understandings of the relation between church and culture. The church's task today is to find a balance so that the differences between these understandings do not become so great that they rule out cooperation, or so small that some people feel they no longer have room in the church.

How Niebuhr Addresses the Dilemma

I find it useful to think of the typology which H. Richard Niebuhr created in *Christ & Culture*, from 1951. Few churches or individuals would recognize themselves in Niebuhr's models. Indeed, those models have often been used to ascribe an identity to others that makes them uncomfortable. Many people have subsequently attempted to elaborate and develop Niebuhr's models in order to find a way of talking about culture and Christ that is meaningful today. But this is not the place to discuss that. Here it is sufficient to note that the relation between church and culture is something that has been seen and discussed continuously throughout Christian history.

In explaining the first model, Niebuhr states that "[t]he first answer to the question of Christ and culture we shall consider is the one that uncompromisingly affirms the sole authority of Christ over the Christian and resolutely rejects culture's claim to loyalty."[60] With some Biblical texts as a starting point, Niebuhr shows how love and faith in Christ are summaries of Christian theology. It is not possible to be a Christian without affirming

---

60. Niebuhr, *Christ & Culture*, 45.

love and Jesus as Christ.[61] At the same time, Niebuhr considers that this positive aspect has a negative counterpart. The world becomes split into two realms, one standing on the side of Christ, the other on the side of evil. There is no blending; one side is good, the other evil. Accordingly, the follower of Christ rejects all that is not on his or her side and focuses instead on the world to come.[62] When Niebuhr examines this position he sees a model that is strong because of the persons who have chosen it. It is filled with persons who ". . . have endured physical and mental suffering in their willingness to abandon homes, property, and the protection of government for the sake of his cause."[63] The persons who populate this model have in many ways changed both church and society, in spite of their dualistic view. In that way they have been influential. Even so, Niebuhr is critical and states that this model has in fact never existed and never will exist in a pure form. We always meet Christ through culture in some form. Niebuhr also points to how readily this model results in a split, not only between Christ and culture, but also between Christ and nature.[64] In this way, Christ becomes something entirely spiritual, with nothing to do with this world. But incarnation speaks otherwise: Christ became one of us—in our cultural setting.[65]

The second model Niebuhr proposes is the Christ of culture. This model expresses a relation between Christ and culture that is fundamentally positive. An example of this model, according to Niebuhr, is the Gnostics in the early church. They did not understand themselves as anything but Christian. But there was a difference that separated them from mainstream Christianity in the early church in that they tried to link the gospel to contemporary knowledge.[66] "They sought to disentangle the gospel from its involvement with barbaric and outmoded Jewish notions about God and history: to raise Christianity from the level of belief to that of intelligent knowledge."[67] At the same time, as Niebuhr says, it was a mystery cult in which ethics played a very different role from Christianity.[68] Proponents

61. Ibid., 46–47.
62. Ibid., 47–48.
63. Ibid., 66.
64. Ibid., 81.
65. Ibid., 80–82.
66. Ibid., 86.
67. Ibid.
68. Ibid., 88–89.

of this model, according to Niebuhr, tend to diminish the gospel. Christ is understood from a cultural point of view and what is not easily compatible with good culture is liable to be ignored. This model has strength and has been able to influence society in many ways. Niebuhr shows that many of its proponents have been knowledgeable people. They have addressed leading groups in society and have thereby meant more than one might think when it comes to spreading Christianity.[69] But Niebuhr also perceives problems with attempts to reconcile Christ and culture. That is sometimes done in such a way that Christ is pictured too simply. Gnostics as well as culture Protestants and others simply pick what they need from the Gospel to form the picture that suits their purpose.

Niebuhr's third model puts Christ above culture and he tries to find a balance between the two by putting the emphasis, not on the relation between them but between Christ and the person. His explanation for this model is that everything is created and structured by God and in that case and if Jesus Christ is the son of God and thereby united with God, there cannot be any real spilt between Christ and culture.[70] Humans must be obedient to God and do that by taking care of themselves and their fellow human beings in the world, which is the cultural world. They must do this inside culture; one cannot live outside culture. For Niebuhr it is important that in this model sin is to be found inside the person, not in what surrounds the person, but it affects what is around. In that way, culture is affected by human sin but is not sinful in itself.[71] Niebuhr sees great advantages with this model but difficulties, too. On the positive side is the possibility of handling both Christ and culture.[72] On the problematic side is the risk of making this synthesis between Christ and culture the goal, not just something with which humans have to live.[73]

The fourth model is Christ and culture in a paradox. To Niebuhr this is largely a development of the third model. Members seek to hold together and at the same time distinguish between Christ and culture.[74] The tension between Christ and culture is incomprehensibly broad and deep–it is a paradox. Niebuhr goes on to say that seeing this as a motif in Christian

69. Ibid., 104–5.
70. Ibid., 117.
71. Ibid., 118–19.
72. Ibid., 122.
73. Ibid., 145–48.
74. Ibid., 149.

thinking may be more correct than seeing it as a model. He exemplifies with reference to St Paul: "The issue of life, as Paul sees it, lies between the righteousness of God and the righteousness of man,"[75] or between God's goodness and the goodness a person seeks in himself.[76] There is a constant understanding that there are tensions in life and a tension between Christ and culture, tensions that one cannot escape but have to live with. "In Christ all things have become new, yet everything remains as it was from the beginning. God has revealed Himself in Christ, but hidden Himself in his revelation; the believer knows the One in whom he has believed, yet walks by faith, not sight."[77]

The fifth and last model, called Christ the transformer of culture, opens up for people's work in culture with the purpose of making it better. Niebuhr considers that this has its roots in some theological concepts: creation, the nature of humans' fall and that for God all things are possible. Creation in this model stands for something good; it centers, not on reconciliation, but on God's good creation. A person belonging to this model puts an emphasis on the Son of God in the very beginning of creation, with a hope for something good. He or she is also concerned with Christ's work to heal people and creation when he walked on this earth. The model does not just use what happened on the cross. It sees a fall, but a fall separated from creation, so that the original nature of the person has been corrupted and in that way culture is corrupted, not by itself, as something evil, but as a result of man's fall.[78] "Hence his culture is corrupted order rather than order for corruption, as it is for dualists. It is perverted good, not evil; or it is evil as perversion, not as badness of being. The problem of culture is therefore the problem of its conversion, not of its replacement by a new creation."[79] In this model, says Niebuhr, life is not lived in accordance with what will come about. What is important and central is God's today. "Eternity means for him less action of God before time and less life with God after time, and more the presence of God in time."[80] For someone with this view, what will

---

75. Ibid., 159–60.
76. Ibid., 160.
77. Ibid., 157.
78. Ibid., 191–93.
79. Ibid., 194.
80. Ibid., 195.

come at the end of time is of little interest; what matters is God's power to transform people and culture in time.[81]

It should be noted that Niebuhr does not see these models as mutually exclusive. None of them appears in real life on its own; they go together and intermingle. Looking for a relation between church or theology and culture is not a quest that can be completed but a constantly ongoing process. If this world is created by God and if Christ is God as well as human, there is a relation between them that every church in every time constantly needs to explore in such a way that both God and culture are taken seriously.

The Situation in the HKBP Seen in Relation to Niebuhr

The HKBP is what one could call a folk church among the Batak people on Sumatra. It is a church with a message about God for the whole of Indonesia; but as it is not allowed to take its mission to the Muslim population, in practice it is a church mainly for Batak people and for non-Christian tribes and other non-Muslim groups.

The most important influence on the HKBP at present probably comes from it existing in a majority Muslim society. This has forced it to withdraw inside its boundaries. Being a public voice in important issues is hard, if not impossible. Neither are other religions permitted to work among or convert Muslims. The space in which the HKBP can function is limited both as to what it can say and do in public and as to whom it can present the gospel.

The situation in Indonesia is constantly becoming harder for Christian churches and the HKBP must at all times consider what it is doing so as not to cause conflicts with the surrounding community. It is a huge church numerically but Christians are just a small minority of the Indonesian population. So there is a constant worry that the situation will become even tenser: there have been some violent clashes recently and churches have been burned; this has happened locally and on a small scale but people are afraid it will escalate. Therefore it is easier—or safer—to "withdraw" from society and concentrate on internal issues. In the present situation it seems best to keep a low profile.

This situation has also led to the HKBP perceiving it to be most important to have a strong government in Indonesia, a government that can guarantee a peaceful future where different groups feel secure and also feel they have the same rights as other groups in society. Stability in the country

---

81. Ibid., 195–96.

is needed as a basis for creating reconciliation and trust between different groups. The religious and political situation in Indonesia prevents the HKBP from acting freely. Being a Christian church in a majority Muslim society, especially in times of political and religious skirmishes, is hazardous for everyone, not just the Christian church. This means that for the HKBP it is most important to act responsibly and that the government sees this. In other words, the HKBP needs to avoid acting provocatively. For the HKPB it is therefore both responsible and relevant to focus on its community rather than having an active, critical voice in society. The government is better off with a church that does not criticize it and the HKBP needs a strong government that safeguards the rights of the church.

The HKBP does not fit easily into one or two of Niebuhr's models. Looking at what the HKBP would like to do—its vision—suggests that it should be placed in a certain model, but looking at how it actually acts points to another outcome. Practical circumstances in the context of the HKBP make it relate to the majority culture in ways it might not have done under other circumstances. The relatively tense situation has made the HKBP move closer to Niebuhr's model number one, though in a modified form. It is relatively closed to the surrounding community, but the reason for this is not a view of Christianity as something that cannot have a fruitful contact with culture, but because it needs to act in this way in order to be a responsible partner in Indonesian society. At the same time, the HKBP seeks in other ways to be closer to model four or five, not least by having a huge social work in its own area, with preschools, schools and hospitals. In that way it hopes to transform society slowly but surely without being seen as a provocateur.

Ethnicity has played an important role in the HKBP from the very beginning. In a sense one could say that the HKBP is an Indonesian folk church. The tense relation between Muslims and Christians does not make the ethnic situation easier to solve. It is easier and safer to stay within the existing boundaries. As previously shown, the relation to the Batak culture is not just old, but also close. Researcher Darwin Lumbantobing expresses this: "So, although they do not admit it, Lutheran churches in Indonesia are ethnic churches. Hence their existence and theology are very close to and greatly influenced by the local culture. Even the problems and challenges of the local churches are dominated by their local culture."[82] This relation to the Batak culture makes the HKBP watch out for syncretism. According to

---

82. Lumbantobing, "Burning Issues in the Lutheran Church in Indonesia," 2.

them, syncretism has been a problem many times through history and the solution has often been not to get rid of it, but to transform it into a Christian version. Other aspects of the traditional culture have been less easy to exclude or transform. An important example is the situation for women, which the HKBP has found it harder to change. In relation to Niebuhr's models, numbers three, four and five are probably most applicable to the HKBP. The church wants to transform culture—as in model five—but this takes time and has to do so in order to avoid a backlash.

Relations with other Christian denominations must be seen in the light of what has been mentioned so far. As the HKBP is banned from recruiting members from the Muslim population, it has to concentrate on the Christian population and the few non-Muslims in Indonesia. New members are hard to get, which makes it all the more important that the church's decisions do not lead to a loss of existing members. Instead of acting so that people leave the church in order to find what they want, it may be better to incorporate things that are popular. This applies in particular to the Charismatic movements in Indonesia.

Mostly United States-based Charismatic movements have been in Indonesia for many years but recently they have been spreading rapidly and affecting the older churches in various ways. Some people have left the HKBP for these movements; others have continued to celebrate in the HKBP and have a dual membership. The HKBP has refrained from opting for a single solution for the whole church, leaving it to each congregation to decide what is wisest in their particular situation. Some parishes have done nothing and gone on as before. Others try to modify their service by using parts of what is to be found in the Charismatic movement's services, such as different types of music, a different style of preaching and so on. Still other parishes have two services, one in a traditional style and the other more charismatic. In this way the HKBP hopes to be a church that will not lose too many members. But as with the IECLB in Brazil, the question is how the HKBP will succeed in making truly pluralistic communities and not just a frame for pluralism, with groups that live in the same frame but never meet one another. In relation to Niebuhr one can describe the HKBP as an open church. Open to new thoughts and new practices, but one can also say that this openness might be forced. Without it, at least some members would probably leave the church. So in relation to Niebuhr an open model is the appropriate description but in a different situation this openness might be less evident.

The HKBP could probably be fitted into all five of Niebuhr's models. A longing to transform, or influence, culture goes hand in hand with a realistic approach to what is feasible when working alongside the major Muslim culture and transforming some and incorporating other aspects of the local Batak culture. That is, vision and practical realities are different things and the pros and cons have to be weighed to find an outcome that leaves the Christian and denominational core values intact but allows the church to function and continue to act in an environment structured by other cultures over which it has no control and frequently has to follow.

The HKBP seems to have something of a split relation to culture. Its particular context, living in a majority Muslim society, limits what it can do in society at large; along with this, it has a special connection to the local Batak culture. It tries to handle the situation by being affirmative of some culture and an alternative to other culture. It is convinced that everyone should hear the gospel and its vision is to be a positive factor in relation to the Muslim community and society in general. In some respects this forces the HKBP against its will to erect barriers around the church. In other respects it gains from these barriers. That is, the HKBP is not a free agent in society but at the same time it obtains approval and support from the government, which sees it as a responsible church in relation to the Muslim majority society.

The Situation in the IECLB Seen in Relation to Niebuhr

The IECLB is probably the church in this study that is working most clearly to include different cultures in one and the same church. The other churches also handle a plurality of cultures in their attempts to be relevant for people, but in the IECLB this has been discussed, structured and taken a bit further. Time has left the IECLB with no chance of doing otherwise. Holding on to the church's traditional role would have led to a gradual marginalization. The IECLB's response to this reality has been to open the church up for, and include, a variety of theological and sociological directions or cultures.

When Niebuhr describes various ways of relating Christ and culture, he notes that they seldom or never exist as separate models but normally interact in one way or another. However, the example of the IECLB shows that to some extent the models essentially have a life of their own. There are different approaches to culture that are distinct and rather easily discerned in the IECLB. For the IECLB, the traditional German, the liberation theological and the Evangelical approaches all have their specific ways of reflecting the relation between Christ and culture. The interesting aspect is probably not the different approaches as such but the fact that they are to be found in one and the same church. This development owes much to exigent circumstances but also to a theological view that the church must be open and inclusive. To be a Lutheran church it must have room for different people, with different views on church, theology and culture.

As has been shown, sometimes—but not often—parishes break away from the IECLB and become free churches with an Evangelical or Charismatic touch. More often they stay with the IECLB and develop a liberationist or Evangelical leaning. This often means that one and the same pastor takes on different roles, functioning at times in a traditional way and at other times in a more Evangelical role. Different groups in the congregation demand different things and the pastor has to deal with them all. This system is working today in the IECLB but the dilemma arises when people and congregations adopt more radical positions. What would happen with the IECLB if different parts of the church become so radical that cooperation between them ceases to be possible? The IECLB handles this situation by allowing local congregations a great deal of freedom in praxis and also by allowing theological and ethical freedom. Opinions and teaching must always be open for discussion. But how much freedom or diversity can a church permit and still manage to hold together?

One could probably say that what is happening in the IECLB has similarities with Niebuhr's model number five, "Christ the transformer of culture." The IECLB wants to center on current developments. They want the church to be open for everyone and human life and wellbeing to be seen as highly central concepts. It follows that the church must be open for diversity, including different views on the relation to culture. It must also leave room for humans to interact and discuss their way forward. And it must allow room for transformation.

INWARD *AND* OUTWARD

Every church needs communities in which the Word of God is heard and bread and wine are shared, a community where people meet, take care of each other and pray for each other. At the same time, no church can function and be content with just this focus. A church must also be directed outwards, into society. Every church needs a core community but that community must be a responsible one, relevant also for a wider society. Inward and outward are two sides of the same coin.

For the IECLB this dilemma is seen in how they try to give room to both liberation theology and Evangelical theology in one and the same church body. The ELCI approaches the dilemma by balancing its outreaching social work with its community building. In the FLM, the dilemma of outwardness and inwardness is seen when the task of being able to grow as a church is put in relation to its will to be an active voice in the political and social landscape.

The HKBP, Indonesia—Boundaries

In the article "Reconciliation in the Indonesian Context," Djohan Effendi discusses the importance of a strong government that can guarantee a peaceful future where different groups feel secure and also feel they have the same rights as other groups in society.

> [In the] Indonesian society being particularly diverse in terms of economics, politics, culture, race ethnicity and religion it will not be easy to achieve reconciliation. These factors are closely interrelated and it is difficult to establish trust not only between government and people, but also among people. Without a government that can effectively keep peace and order, without the implementation of the rule of law and without mutual trust and respect there can be no reconciliation. Genuine and long-lasting reconciliation, therefore, has to be developed through sincere and real cooperation between local leaders and local authorities at the grassroots level.[83]

Whatever one thinks of this situation, it is the reality the HKBP has to live with. The trust between different groups and religions does not exist automatically; it has to be safeguarded by constant mutual work by all actors and must also be anchored in a strong government which can ensure that agreements and laws are respected by everyone. The consequences differ for different groups in Indonesian society. For the HKBP this means that barriers are erected that prevent the church from acting freely. Reaching in to its own community is one thing; neither is reaching out in a social sphere problematic. But reaching out into what could be understood as a political sphere or into the domains of other religions could be catastrophic, leaving the HKBP with no chance of performing its mission as a church to its full extent.

83. Effendi, "Reconciliation in the Indonesian Context," 115.

The ILCO, Costa Rica—Community as a Way to Reach Out

The goal of the ILCO is to be an open church with no walls, a church that includes as many people as possible, regardless of their views, actions and beliefs. According to them a church must always take an active part in society, listening to the call of whoever it meets.

During its relatively brief history the ILCO has developed into a church with the explicit goal of creating communities that are not uniform. It is an outspoken goal that people must be able to join the church without having to change. It is a church that wants to be open for everyone as they are, not as the church might want them to be. It is also a church with a radical view on social work in general and who's voice the church should be in society. But it also sees the problems with this radical openness, such as the tense relations it sometimes entails with other churches as well as with society in general because most people outside the church regard what the ILCO is doing as strange and hard to understand. Members of the ILCO are also aware that for some people the focus of the church's work is not just strange but can actually function as an excluding mechanism. People who might sympathize with Lutheran ethics and theology on a general level may hesitate to join the ILCO because of its position on issues that Costa Rican society in general finds radical.

How Moltmann Addresses the Dilemma

Jürgen Moltmann's *The Church in the Power of the Spirit*, published in the mid-1970s,[84] is the third part of a trilogy of which the others are *The Crucified God*[85] and *Theology of Hope*.[86] *The Church in the Power of the Spirit* concentrates on church and Spirit and the other two deal with resurrection and the cross. All of them are concerned with the main elements in theology, but from different angles. The purpose of the following is to show that the inward and the outward are equally important in ecclesiology, Christian theology, and church life. Neither of these concepts can take advantage of the other in such a way that the counterpart becomes less important. The inward and the outward directions must be there together and complement each other.

---

84. Moltmann, *Church in the Power of the Spirit*.
85. Moltmann, *Crucified God*.
86. Moltmann, *Theology of Hope*.

Moltmann begins by saying that the church has obligations before God, humans and the future, all three. When the church closes itself to any one of the three, it will eventually cease to be a church.[87] In different ways he then discusses the essence and task of the church in the world, but all the time with a perspective that holds together God, humanity and the future in a way which makes it clear that the church not only has to be open for God and humanity, but also responsible for the world here and now. For Moltmann, ecclesiology starts from the view that the church cannot be described without Christ. The church starts with Christ and ends with eschatology and has to be understood in those relations.[88] The church lives in a time in between and is constantly on the move towards the coming of the kingdom. It is on the move because of Christ, who is the starting point, but at the same time it is filled with the hope of what is to come. In that space, in between, we find the church. "The lordship of Christ is the church's sole, and hence all-embracing, determining factor. It can neither be shared nor restricted" says Moltmann.[89] Therefore he argues that Christ is the subject for the church and that all that is said about the church must be seen from the perspective of Christ. All that could be said about Christ could also be said about the church. But Moltmann goes further: ". . . yet the statement about Christ is not exhausted by the statement about the church because it also goes further, being directed towards the messianic kingdom which the church serves."[90] Thus, Moltmann's view of the church is based on Christology, the life of Christ, his ministry and work, but also based on eschatology. The church of today knows the future with the help of the Spirit. In that way the church is a part of God's future through the presence of the Spirit, "[t]hat through which we perceive the history and promise of Christ, that through which we become aware of the coming rule of God in word and sacrament and church, and through which we enter into the fellowship of the history of the triune God—this perception, this awareness and his fellowship must itself be termed God, the Holy Spirit."[91] It is the Spirit that makes the church function; the Spirit gives the power and makes the church move forward.

87. Moltmann, *Church in the Power of the Spirit*, 2.
88. Ibid., 19–20.
89. Ibid., 5.
90. Ibid., 6.
91. Ibid., 28.

The Spirit calls on everyone to be a part of this church. For Moltmann it is important to understand the church in such a way that when a person is called, he or she is called to something more than being an individual listening to the Word and celebrating Eucharist. In the Creed one can read about the "communion of saints;" for Luther this meant, according to Moltmann, the congregation or the Christian people who live in relation to each other and who take responsibility for each other.[92] This is true and very important for Moltmann, but he adds that it is equally true and important that even if Word and sacrament constitute the fellowship, something important is missing if the fellowship is not constituted by love.[93] He finds the missing part in the third article in the Barmen declaration: the community of brethren.

> "The Christian church is the community of brethren." A community of brethren lives in the spirit of brotherliness, showing its fellowship with God's Son, 'the first-born among many brethren' (Rom 8:29), through a brotherly common life. This goes further than an assembly of believers for the purpose of proclaiming the gospel and partaking in the sacraments (although that is a source) and embraces the whole of life, our dealings with one another, our representation for others and our common actions. This "community of brethren" means the new, visible way of life. In the New Testament this is often contrasted with social conditions in the surrounding world. In the community of brethren there is no more lordship or slavery: "It shall not be so among you" (Matt 20:26). In the community of brethren the greed for possessions and the claim to personal property came to an end.... The community of brethren proclaims the kingdom of God through its way of life, which provides an alternative to the life of the world surrounding it.[94]

In that way the church is more for Moltmann than just a collection of individuals; it is what he calls—instead of brotherhood—a fellowship of friends. Friendship is the term he uses to express relations in the church. They are relations in which you love in freedom, he argues. It is a free choice to be a friend of someone and the friendship has its roots in Christ freely giving his life for his friends.[95] It is a fellowship of friends who gather

---

92. Ibid., 314.
93. Ibid., 315.
94. Ibid., 315–16.
95. Ibid., 316.

together, take care of each other and help each other, but they do not do this as a sect that withdraws from the world. Rather the fellowship of friends has a task in the world. And the task is to be a church of Jesus Christ, a missionary church, an ecumenical church and a political church.[96] The church lives with the hope of the future and in all that it does it tries to reflect the coming kingdom. It sees every person, no matter who they are, and it struggles to mend the creation. The church is a community made for action.

> The visible coming together of visible people in a special place to do something particular stands at the centre of the church. Without the actual, visible procedure of meeting together there is no church. That is why everything in the church is concentrated on this procedure. Where the community gathers round the gospel and the Lord's table, it becomes recognizable in the world and unmistakably the people of Christ, the messianic community of the coming kingdom. In and through its actual assemblies it is free from those political powers and laws which the Barmen Declaration, article II, assigned to "the godless ties of the world." In the fellowship of Christ it becomes a community capable of action. The facts are simple enough: without assembly no fellowship, without fellowship no freedom, without freedom no capacity for action. Because the invitation of the gospel and the invitation to the messianic banquet are open, and reach further than the group of those who are assembled, this group can never form a closed circle. It is open, and will practice this openness for other people through evangelization and practical acts of liberation. If the assembled community were not to be an "open church" it would neither be the church of Christ nor the people of the coming kingdom. But if its openness to the world meant that it no longer gathered together, then it would not be a community or a people.[97]

To be able to be a community of friends with the living hope of the coming kingdom it needs, according to Moltmann, to be a fellowship in real praxis.[98] And to be able to establish that true fellowship in praxis the church must be something more than a community of the baptized; it must be a community of choice. And this community gets its strength from the gospel, baptism, the Lord's supper and worship to be able to act. For Moltmann all of them are needed to form and maintain a fellowship, but at the

---

96. Ibid., 4–18.
97. Ibid., 334.
98. Ibid., 317.

same time they must be understood in an open way. The gospel is heard in different ways, but always offered to everyone. Baptism "demonstrates the dawn of the rule of God in personal life and the common conversion to the future of that rule."[99] But it is also an invitation to work outside the community.[100] The Lord's supper must be truly open, says Moltmann, "[i]t is not the openness of this invitation, it is the restrictive measures of the churches which have to be justified before the face of the crucified Jesus."[101] In Christian worship the community renews its hope in the kingdom, God's love and openness to the world.[102] By taking part in sacrament and worship, one's remembrance of Christ is actualized and thereby the community's fellowship will be strengthened.

As said, fellowship in the church is not there for its own sake, it is a fellowship for the world. For Moltmann this is important. He points to the difficult times in which we live and says, "[i]n this crisis faith means courage to be, the affirmation of life, loyalty to the earth."[103] Being loyal to Christ means having a task in this world.

> In this context Christianity in the world can be expected to overcome the fatal loss of courage with its *passion for living*. It can be expected to make life possible in face of the threat of death through the power of hope given by its faith. It can be expected to put a stop to the shifting of suffering on to others, through the capacity for suffering of its own love; and—contrary to the "struggle for existence"—to build solidarity within the frontiers of existence.[104]

The strong Christian community of friends is there because it has a task, to help heal the world. In saying that it is important to remember that the church is not the only agent through which God acts in this world. The Spirit guides the church and strengthens it, but the church is not the keeper of the Spirit; according to Moltmann, the Spirit is to be found everywhere. God meets his world in many different ways and the church is one of them, but not the only one. "It is not the church that has a mission of salvation

---

99. Ibid., 226.
100. Ibid., 242.
101. Ibid., 246.
102. Ibid., 261.
103. Ibid., 165.
104. Ibid., 167.

to fulfil to the world; it is the mission of the Son and the Spirit through the Father that includes the church, creating a church as it goes on its way."[105]

> The church participates in Christ's messianic mission and in the creative mission of the Spirit. We cannot therefore say what the church is in all circumstances and what it comprises in itself. But we can tell the church happens. The phrase "the church is present where . . ." used in article VII of the Augsburg Confession and in article III of the Barmen Declaration, is a correct one, but it cannot be restricted merely to "true proclamation" and "a right administration of the sacraments." Both are included, yet we shall have to say more comprehensively: the church is present wherever "the manifestation of the Spirit" [1 Cor 12:7] takes place.[106]

The Situation in the HKBP Seen in Relation to Moltmann

As seen in the reflection on the dilemma of being an alternative to culture *and* being affirmative of culture in relation to the HKBP, living in a Muslim majority society also affects this dilemma. In everything it does the HKBP needs to bear in mind that it has boundaries which most other churches do not have.

Moltmann was writing in a very different situation, where people and churches could act as they wished. If one disregarded this and applied Moltmann's reflections to the work of the HKBP, it would be easy to say that the HKBP does not see its task in Indonesian society as it should. For Moltmann the church has a task that can be described in various ways, but it should be a church of Christ, a missionary church, an ecumenical church and a political church. One could say that for Moltmann the church is a community of brothers and sisters, but also a community made for action. The church should be a fellowship that transforms society. This the HKBP cannot do; the political scene is closed to it and doing otherwise would probably entail enormous costs for people and the church itself.

What can be and is done by the HKBP—and what Moltmann requires—is the creation of prosperous church communities where the Word of God is heard and bread and wine are shared. But also that these church communities take a huge social responsibility for people by providing education, health care and so on. The HKBP is the largest Lutheran church in Indonesia and is also numerically big, making it a very important factor

---

105. Ibid., 64.
106. Ibid., 65.

in the social sphere, especially on Sumatra. For Moltmann all this is important. A church needs to invite to a community that relates humans to God, but also to a community where people take care of each other and demonstrate responsibility for each other and for creation.

However, for Moltmann this is just the first step. A community must be there, no church can function without people who meet, listen to God and try to meet each other's needs; but as said, that community also has a wider function, namely to transform. This is clear to the HKBP but doing it is not easy. The situation is liable to be seen as insoluble, which makes it a real dilemma. How to be a church in its true sense, when one cannot live up to the Gospels' expectations? If Moltmann asks for a church that creates communities of love for the sake of transforming society, how is one to live up to this when the political scene is closed?

Part of the answer for the HKBP has been to be an active agent when it comes to social work among its members; transforming society by being an example of how a good and prosperous society could be built. The answer has also included being in constant dialogue with the Muslim majority society and its leaders. Building a trustworthy, solid ground for both parties. A ground that hopefully could lead to a more relaxed relationship. Hopefully making room—in the future—for the HKBP to act without the current barriers. By doing this the HKBP also provides an answer that could be interpreted as in line with Moltmann. Namely, that the church does not have to do everything itself. The transformation of society is not solely up to the church. The Spirit is not only found inside the church and the church is not the keeper of the Spirit. The Spirit guides the church but is also to be found elsewhere. The church can therefore be confident that God is also working outside its borders. This means that, instead of transforming society on its own, the HKBP can, in various ways, help other agents in Indonesian society to do good and thereby hope it is aiding the Spirit outside the HKBP's domain.

The Situation in the ILCO Seen in Relation to Moltmann

From Moltmann's point of view, the relation between the inward and the outward should not be hard to handle in a relevant way. The inward and the outward are equally important and neither can take advantage of the other in such a way that the latter becomes less important. One can say that the church has obligations to both God and humans, so if it shuts itself off from either of them it will ultimately cease to be a church. In everything it does the church must therefore always have a perspective that holds God and humans together in such a way that it is clearly open not only to God but also to humans and in everything it does is responsible for the world here and now as well as for the world to come.

But while there is always some sort of a relation between the inward and the outward in every church, it is not a fixed relation; it can in fact look very different from church to church and from time to time, but still be a healthy relation. At the same time, it can easily turn into an unhealthy relation whereby the church risks becoming introverted. If all its energy and interest are directed inwards, it may gradually turn into a sect with no concern for the wellbeing of the rest of society. Similarly, every church runs the risk of putting too much emphasis on the outward direction and gradually turning into something other than a church. The relation between the inward and the outward must always be examined, understood and discussed so that these extremes are less likely to happen. This dual, simultaneous direction—inward and outward—is highly important for Moltmann, but while it is theologically important it could be difficult to achieve in practice.

Costa Rican culture is male-dominated and value-conservative. In this context the ILCO has created a church with values and behaviors that in many ways are the opposite of what is seen in society in general. The ILCO tries to "see" and "hear" people who are normally not "seen" or "heard," such as women, homosexuals and the very poor. It empowers the people it meets and tries to create a platform for them in society.

The ILCO's members and sympathizers talk of themselves as a church, but also as a movement which has an agenda for changing things in society of which they disapprove. Members of the ILCO say they want to see themselves as a sign of hope for those who need it. Things do not have to continue as they are; an oppressive culture and an unequal society can change, even if that takes time and effort. For the ILCO, Christian life should be lived in society, not in a Christian ghetto. This outreaching dimension is what the ILCO is known for in Costa Rican society. At the same time the ILCO is aware, just like Moltmann, that a church must have two directions, inwards and outwards. Besides having an outward direction, a church must be based on a community of friends. That is, a baptized community that shares the Lord's supper. A community of people who take care of each other and empower each other in a constant struggle for the kingdom to come. Building this type of church community and also reaching out is what the ILCO tries to do in its different church communities and places for pastoral work. But this could create a dilemma for the ILCO. The strong emphasis on social questions makes it relatively hard to build prosperous, growing communities. Members of the ILCO seem to be aware that their special focus on what they are doing might be understood as strange or even non-Christian by other churches and by many people in Costa Rica. It might then seem difficult to combine the two directions, inward and outward. However, for the ILCO this does not appear to be a problem. They consider that a faith without action is not a true faith. By joining the ILCO you become not just a member of a church, but of a church with a very special vocation. The ILCO's major tasks have been to give a voice to the voiceless, power to the powerless and so on, in an attempt to be faithful to the gospel. Members say that the ILCO strives to be a sign of God's kingdom in a practical way and do this by trying not to separate the political from the religious. The ILCO is a church with a clear vision that God's work is to be found, not just in the church but in society at large. So what for many other churches would probably be a huge dilemma—having problems with growth on account of active social work—calling for reformulations of what is being done, does not seem to be a dilemma in the same way for the ILCO. They are content to remain a small group with a large voice and widespread social work.

What they are doing very much resembles what Moltmann asks for. It is in society that the ILCO has a task, not primarily in the small group or community. The inward direction is there, of course, but as a way of fulfilling the purpose of directing the church outwards. Perhaps the situation would have looked otherwise if the ILCO had another and longer history, a larger organization and more members to be responsible to. With its small size and relatively short history, the ILCO is relatively free from ties and thereby able to act freely.

The question of growth might be a dilemma for most churches but not for the ILCO. A real dilemma for the ILCO is, however, that its rather strong focus on social reality makes it necessary to be constantly aware of what makes its community a church, not just an NGO. They have a background as a movement and work closely today with other movements and NGOs; indeed, people outside the ILCO often see it as an NGO. In order to avoid becoming just a movement and not a church, it has been important to accentuate some features of the church. One is the decision to ordain a bishop instead of having a chairman, another is their efforts to maintain the standard of training for the priesthood and their many important international and ecumenical contacts. All of this tends to strengthen the core community and so helps to balance the inward and outward directions, in the way Moltmann talks.

A FEW REFLECTIONS

This chapter illustrates how the churches are constantly evolving. They are being built, negotiated and renegotiated in a never-ending process. It shows that it is the churches' histories and contexts that are in the foreground no matter what dilemmas they confront. It also prompts the reflection that Lutheranism, or themes that are often referred to as parts of the Lutheran heritage, tend not to be articulated openly. It could be said that the material suggests that all five churches have some difficulty in expressing the role of Luther or Lutheranism. It is striking how seldom Luther or Lutheranism are mentioned explicitly. This "tacit" role for Lutheranism makes it hard to tell how the Lutheran heritage or Lutheran theology are used or discussed. Ethnicity, history, context, the presence of other religions and many other factors are frequently discussed and the churches do not just talk about those factors, they also do their best to relate to them when handling the dilemmas. It is interesting that the Lutheran heritage is seldom mentioned as a tool for dealing with the dilemmas. However, while the material contains little evidence of an explicit, outspoken Lutheranism, it does provide some hints or interpretations of Lutheranism.

Responsible, Relevant, and Authentic

Different interpretations of Lutheranism are discussed by Professor Vitór Westhelle in the article "Transfiguring Lutheranism: Being Lutheran in New Contexts." He argues that as newer churches have normally been founded by missionary efforts and colonialism, they have often inherited the older churches' agenda. Lutheranism has therefore—even in more recently established churches—often served to conserve ideas from the past. It has, to some extent, become a denomination that represents what existed long ago in northern Europe. So how can Lutheranism function as something whereby experiences from another time and another place are transformed to the world of today? His answer is that while Lutheranism does contain motives and doctrines which could be of great importance, it is crucial that they help solve real questions for real people, also today. In the case of Luther, justification by grace unlocked what had kept him in fear and despair. But, says Westhelle, that key is only good if it succeeds in opening the locks that keep humans captive today.[107]

What the churches in this study are doing when handling the dilemmas can be interpreted along the lines Westhelle proposes, namely as a search for keys that can unlock what is binding them today. To some extent one could say they are standing in a tradition of *semper reformanda*. If Luther's main concern was where to find a merciful God, the churches in this study wonder how can they be seen and understood as responsible and relevant in peoples' search to free themselves from what ties them down. Ties that, as the material shows, often stem from history or context and often relate to poverty, gender, sexuality, colonization, relations with other religions or other similar things. By responsible I mean that the churches would like to act in such a way that both they and society benefit from what they are doing. By relevant I mean that the churches are seeking to act in such a way that people, in their own church or in society in general, perceive what is happening as relevant. Of course, what one church understands as being a responsible and relevant way of acting can differ from the other churches' understanding, depending on the context in which they are located and other factors. As we have seen, how to be responsible and relevant differs enormously between a folk church on Iceland and a minority church in Indonesia. Or between a very small, but socially active, church in Costa Rica and a rapidly growing church in a politically turbulent Madagascar.

However, besides striving to act responsibly and relevantly, in a *semper reformanda* way, it seems as if the churches want to do so authentically. In their praxis they strive to act in such a way that they themselves understand what they are doing as in keeping with whom they understand themselves to be (e.g., Lutherans). This means that they also have a more confessional understanding of their heritage and of who they are. It is seldom expressed explicitly, but the material shows that all five churches are using the Lutheran tradition when handling the dilemmas, but they do it in a way that is not always clearly expressed. It seems more to be a ground on which they stand.

---

107. Westhelle, "Transfiguring Lutheranism."

5

Tradition as a Tool

From the previous chapter it is evident that the churches in this study are constantly evolving and finding the way forward by handling the dilemmas they meet. This they do in what can be understood as a *semper reformanda* way. However, they are also striving to act authentically, trying to handle the upcoming situations in what can be understood as confessional ways. This chapter presents a tentative interpretation of this. The material is too vague to support a single interpretation. What is said is simply a set of suggestions or proposals, not definite claims.

This is not the place for a normative statement about what Lutheran means or what should be included in a confessional Lutheran theology; that has been a subject for numerous discussions and distinctions. As Professor Niels Henrik Gregersen writes,

> [L]utheran thinking has often been caught up in a theological essentialism searching for the "kerygma" (Rudolf Bultmann), "the eternal message" (Paul Tillich), "the Word in the words," and so on. This essentialism goes hand in hand with a theological minimalism that is characterized by a combination of strong general assertions with a correspondingly thin bone of content.[1]

However, a few examples of what is often said to belong to the core of the Lutheran tradition, examples that also occur in the present material, will be discussed to see how the churches' foundations could be understood as their Lutheran heritage. These are only some of the many examples in the material.

1. Gregersen, "Introduction," 6.

Here I have chosen to look briefly at four examples: the doctrine of the two kingdoms, the doctrine of universal priesthood, Luther's teaching on vocation, and the doctrine of justification.

DOCTRINE OF THE TWO KINGDOMS

The Two Kingdoms Doctrine cannot be clearly related to Luther himself. Still, it is something that can be used to give an overview or a simplified view of how Luther and his contemporary fellow theologians perceived the relationship between salvation and society. Moreover, in the twentieth century it played a political role during the Nazi regime in Germany by being used by pro-Nazi theologians to legitimize what was happening.[2] Because of the use or misuse of the doctrine during the past hundred years, the Two Kingdoms Doctrine is vigorously debated today.

Briefly, the Two Kingdoms Doctrine aims to teach that God relates to the world in two ways: through the realm of the world and through the realm of the Christian community. In the former way, God maintains the creation and people living together. In the latter, God grants salvation from sin and death. This should not to be understood as one kingdom being by God and the other not. Rather both are there according to the will of God. That is, the realm of the world is also willed by God. So people have to obey their rulers at the same time as society has to be ruled in such a way that the will of God is evident.[3]

It is easy to see that this can readily lead to misunderstandings and abuses, often leading Lutheran Churches to remain silent on social and political issues. Lutheran churches have indeed tended to be a weak prophetic voice in society. They have often been apolitical, at least in praxis.[4] It is clear that the Two Kingdoms Doctrine has been—and sometime is—used to hinder the church from criticizing what is happening in society[5]. The opposite also occurs—more and more so today—problematizing and making room for a socially engaged Lutheranism that sees the public good and is engaged in social and political issues.[6] As said, history in general depicts a weak relation between Lutheran churches and social activities but there

---

2. Lohse, *Martin Luther's Theology*, 315.
3. Ibid., 314–24.
4. Isaak, "Church's Prophetic Witness," 148–149.
5. See for example: Chung et al., *Liberating Lutheran Theology*, 46–52.
6. See for example: Nürnberger, *Martin Luther's Message for Us Today*, 243–76 or Altmann, *Luther and Liberation*, 69–83.

have been exceptions and things can change in the future. Some contrary interpretations are presented by Professor Antti Raunio in "Luther's Social Theology in the Contemporary World."

> Lutheranism is often seen as socially disinterested, but this stereotype cannot hold true. Lutheranism is known for the idea that faith frees the human being to serve the neighbor in love. Luther defines the love of neighbor as a striving for the good of another. The self is freed from striving for personal good and gain. Luther often describes neighborly love as a love that aims solely to fulfill the neighbor's need. The neighbor's need is precisely the point at which Luther begins to determine the good. Luther does not start with the person's effort to attain and guarantee her own good but turns the attention to the neighbor.[7]

Raunio considers that separating the personal good from the communal good is likely to have serious consequences and goes on to ask whether a community of mutual service and love can be realized. In his opinion, such a community is for Luther a natural outcome of his theology and has its beginning here and now but everyone must constantly strive for it in order to bring it about.[8]

The churches in this study often appear to consider that having a social commitment which goes beyond the sphere of the church and extends into society is of the utmost importance. Their arguments for what they are doing differ and so do their possibilities of achieving it but social commitment seems to be important. One could say that what these churches are doing is being builders and, in some cases, constructive critics. They are all building, not just faith communities, but social structures and institutions, for instance preschools, schools, universities, hospitals, and orphanages. Many of them are in fact well-known for creating such social structures and institutions that benefit society as a whole. Moreover, some of them are also what could be labeled constructive critics. That is, besides building for the good of society, they are constructively criticizing what they see as unjust structures in terms of economy, gender, race and many other things.

As mentioned earlier, the main difference between them as regards their ability to be constructive critics as well as builders is not solely a matter of different interpretations of what the Lutheran heritage means to them or of interpretations of Christian theology, but is deeply informed

---

7. Raunio, "Luther's Social Theology," 216.
8. Ibid., 227.

by contextual facts. Those churches that can have a free voice in society without this leading to larger problems are also using their voice to criticize what they see as unjust. This is evident in the ILCO in Costa Rica, which by its small size has little to lose at the same time as the country's political stability makes it relatively safe to voice an opinion that is not shared by the majority. The churches that face a more troublesome political, social or religious situation seem to act mainly as builders because they naturally fear that if they were to criticize what they see in society, they might lose their ability to grow and to build. An example of this is the FLM in Madagascar, which does a great deal of social work but is more reluctant to criticize the regime. This does not mean that the churches which have a steady, critical voice in society would act otherwise if their situation required them to criticize a repressive regime that could react by causing them trouble. It is rather an observation of the current situation. The churches that see little risk in having a political voice have such a voice; those that fear this would be costly seem not to.

DOCTRINE OF THE UNIVERSAL PRIESTHOOD

First Peter 2:9 reads: "But you are a chosen race, a royal priesthood, a holy nation, God's own people, in order that you may proclaim the mighty acts of him who called you out of darkness into his marvelous light." For Luther this verse was important for his arguments against papal power over secular authorities, as well as for his arguments about power in the church. Every person has a relation to God and that relation does not have to be mediated through someone else. Priesthood is important for Luther, but just as a question of order. Every church needs an order and therefore some people are singled out to preach and deliver the sacraments. But that does not turn them into something which baptism has not already made them. Baptism and faith are all that are needed and there is therefore a direct line between God and humans. There is no need for a religious order or religious authorities to stand between God and humankind, other than as a question of order.[9]

The doctrine of a universal priesthood has had a tremendous impact on Lutheran churches during history, often giving religious freedom to the individual and constructing church organizations that could help the individual carry that freedom in a responsible way. But while the doctrine of the universal priesthood has been a source of individual religious rights,

9. Wriedt, "Luther's Theology," 101–2.

churches have not always readily embraced it, as Professor Allen G. Jorgenson argues in the article "Contours of the Common Priesthood." There he shows how radical the doctrine is but also notes that Luther as well as Lutheran churches have generally failed to do that radicalness justice. Jorgenson sees examples of this in churches' treatment of gays and lesbians, in the frequent inability to make churches truly inclusive communities and, not least, in the question of the ordination of women.[10]

> Luther's treatment of the priesthood of all believers was dogmatically rich enough to embrace the constitutive, missionary, and mutual identities of the church. In fact, however, the recurrence of familial language in Lutheranism too often reprises patriarchal and parochial patterns of thought. This is sometimes seen in Luther, who denied women a voice at the baptismal font, pulpit, and altar—save in the case of an emergency—and thereby rendered one gender impotent. This proviso is an assault to Luther's own theology of ministry: if all are priests, then that reality should gain visibility and voice in the living world: While not every priest can be ordained, an ordered ministry that fails to mirror the diversity of the priesthood has failed itself.[11]

So in what way is this doctrine evident in the present material? The churches are deeply concerned with how best to listen to and handle what is happening around them in a relevant and responsible way. The gospel is constantly interpreted and different things are highlighted at different times, depending on what they are trying to solve. This is an ongoing process, which means that the churches are constantly evolving and constantly creating local answers with the aid of the tools they choose to use. But as said earlier, they are seldom totally free to construct these local theologies as they wish. The local theologies in this material are always compromises as each church tries to handle dilemmas and at the same time allow for a variety of internal and external factors. But as they handle their different situations, a few things clearly stand out as important: education for the individual, and democracy. All the churches seem to have an understanding of the value of education. Education and schooling are central for them all in their attempts to provide people with tools for acting responsibly and formulating constructive criticism of things they encounter in life, church and society. The democratic structures of the churches are also important,

---

10. Jorgenson, "Contours of the Common Priesthood," 249–65.
11. Ibid., 264.

with room for voices that differ in their background, general opinion, gender, education, and political opinion. This means that the individual has both the right and the possibility, no matter who he or she is, to contribute and act responsibly. This is probably clearest in the ELCI in Iceland, being a democratic folk church, but is also to be found in the other churches, not least in the ILCO in Costa Rica with its strong emphasis on giving the poor and exploited a voice in society. In the FLM in Madagascar it is visible in the Shepherds movement; the FLM has a rather strict hierarchy but in the Shepherds movement this is in some way turned upside down and women have a leading role.

At the same time as education and democracy can be said to be important in this material, there is also evidence of what Allen G. Jorgensen saw above, namely that some Lutheran churches have a long way to go before a universal priesthood is in full function. Even if education and democracy are present, it does not follow that all the parameters of the universal priesthood are to be found. As Jorgensen points out, ordination of women, constructing inclusive communities and creating a truly democratic structure are examples of matters where churches sometimes have difficulty in fulfilling the intentions of the universal priesthood. But there is evidence of an endeavor or an ambition.

THE VOCATION

Lutheran theology does not only disallow a distinction between people when it comes to the doctrine of the universal priesthood. It also sees it as important that everyone has a vocation and that their vocations cannot be said to differ in importance. Luther argues against the religious elite seeing what they are doing as more important than other things, for example what a baker or a carpenter are doing. Professor Carter Lindberg writes:

> Luther rejected flight into self-chosen religious callings of clericalism, and called people to serve others in the web of relationships where they live. We are to do, Luther asserted; what God commands not what we fancy God would like. Here, again, Luther focused on "the ordinary." The perennial temptation of the religious person is the desire to do "important" things rather than sweep the floor, change diapers, and do the dishes. Luther's point, however; is that we are not called to self-chosen extraordinary tasks, but rather to service in the world.[12]

12. Lindberg, "Luther's Struggle," 170.

A vocation relates to creation in that it is God who calls people to different tasks to make the earth a possible place to live on. There is no qualitative difference between vocations. Secular vocations are worth neither less nor more than a priestly vocation. It is not what is done that is important but the faith that accompanies the vocation. It is also important to remember that whatever my vocation is, it is always directed to my fellow human beings. People do not just have a vocation in what they do for a living; they have a vocation from God in everything they do, for example as a father or a mother, as a son or a daughter.[13] Luther's teaching on vocation has played an important role in history but in the twentieth century it has been rightfully criticized, not least for conserving social and political structures.[14]

If vocation is considered as a way of making the world stay alive, all five churches are involved in doing this. But a problematized approach to vocation is not to be found in every case. As said earlier, all five churches see education as important and aim to make it possible for people to take on the vocation they feel they should have. Education enables people to pursue vocations which would otherwise have been closed to them. The churches try to lower barriers but do so most clearly with respect to financial obstacles. Cultural barriers and hindrances based on gender are not addressed to the same extent in every case. One could say that their interpretations of the Lutheran heritage seem to be largely in line with the general culture, and when this is not the case, the church has little to lose by going its own way. This is seen in the small ILCO's progressive work, in the Icelandic folk church ELCI and in the IECLB in Brazil, for example with its two women's organizations. A new cultural atmosphere calls for changes in the church.

DOCTRINE OF JUSTIFICATION

> The doctrine of justification is not simply one doctrine among others but—as Luther declares—the basic and chief article of faith with which the church stands or falls, and on which its entire doctrine depends. The doctrine of justification is "the summary of Christian doctrine," "the sun which illuminates God's holy church." It is the unique possession of Christianity and "distinguishes our religion from all others." The doctrine of justification preserves the

---

13. Hägglund, *Teologins historia*, 211–12.

14. See for example Lagerquist and Riswold, "Historical and Theological Legacies," 24–26.

church. If we lose this doctrine, we also lose Christ and the church; for then no Christian understanding remains. What is at stake in this doctrine is the decisive question as how man can continue to stand before God.[15]

As well understood from Paul Althaus, this is the primary doctrine for Luther. It is rooted in Augustine and the teaching of inherited sin. Men and women live their lives turned away from God in a way that human efforts cannot repair. It is through the righteousness of Christ that men and women are justified by grace. Or maybe better, men and women are seen by God as justified by faith for the sake of Christ. But that does not mean this has been done once and for all. Every person has to struggle every day; simultaneously righteous and sinner.[16]

While Lutheranism cannot be understood without this doctrine, interpretations of it are sometimes understood as too academic; they have had little to say to most people. Professor Wanda Deifeldt mentions this in relation to an LWF meeting in Brazil in 1988.

> ... some of the participants after having heard a condensed, rather heavy lecture on the topic of Luther's theology in the context of the developing world asked quite bluntly, who besides Lutheran theologians would turn to Luther's theology and ask for the Lutheran interpretation on any subject before getting involved in the daily struggles of human existence, the struggle for survival, to make ends meet, to make a decent living, to assure the family's well being.[17]

In the article "Justification and Society," Reinhard Höppner discusses the problems that can arise when a doctrine becomes all too disconnected from the lives of ordinary people and churches. But he also gives examples of, and discusses, what the Doctrine of Justification could mean in the world of today? It could include matters such as reconciliation with the sinner, which calls for everybody's involvement, not least churches'. It could represent a critique of a society built on everybody's attempts to have power at the expense of others. And a critique of a society in which everything must be correct right from the start, instead of letting people try and try again. It is not for making mistakes that a person is condemned, nor is it

---

15. Althaus, *Theology of Martin Luther*, 224.
16. Ibid., 224–50.
17. Deifeldt, "Relevance of the Doctrine of Justification," 33.

by what is accomplished that a person is saved. Therefore people have the ability and the right to try again and again to build a better world.[18]

Examples of the Doctrine of Justification that relate to interpretations like this are to be found in all five churches. Examples that point to a more classical dogmatic interpretation or discussion are harder to find. The doctrine is often used as a way to free people from cultural pressures. In the HKBP in Indonesia this is, for example, seen in relation to how they are trying to find theological arguments for how to relate to culture: what has to be abandoned, what can be reformulated and what can stay as it is? Culture no longer binds people in a negative way with things that must be done, but can rather be used in a freer, more liberating way. The same can be seen in the FLM in Madagascar. People no longer have to please the spirits, they are free to act and handle without taking the traditional culture into account. As for the ILCO in Costa Rica, their eagerness to be a sign and a church without walls could be seen as their way to handle the Doctrine of Justification. They know their mission is complicated, with a large risk of failure, but that does not matter because it is not by being successful that they are redeemed. They are redeemed by faith, which leaves them free to act. The same goes for the persons they invite; they are invited, not to be changed from whom they are, but to live by faith.

A PROBLEMATIC DISCREPANCY

There seems to be a discrepancy in the churches between a more explicit *semper reformanda* understanding of the Lutheran heritage and a more hidden, often tacit, confessional understanding. In theory, the *semper reformanda* understanding licenses the churches to evolve in relation to what they need to handle, whereas how they are evolving is based on the confessional understanding of their heritage. Still, a discrepancy between a *semper reformanda* understanding and a confessional understanding of the heritage—as seen among the churches in the study—could have important consequences. One consequence could be that if the Lutheran heritage is not handled carefully, it could take the form of an ideological approval of what the churches want to do when handling the dilemmas, giving a Lutheran green light to decisions and actions. There is little visible evidence in the material that the churches are using their Lutheran heritage in a more constructive or critical way, as a means of conducting a critical dialogue with context and circumstances in the context of a likewise critical dialogue

18. Höppner, "Justification and Society," 31–32.

with theological history. This could be seen as a critique of the churches in this study—and in some way it is—but at the same time it is a critique that probably applies to a greater or lesser degree to every church. Having a serious dialogue with history as a way of moving forward is both difficult and rare.

A Need for a Critical Dialogue with Tradition

Professor and former archbishop Rowan Williams addresses this question in his book *Why Study the Past?* The diversified history of the Christian church shows how people have constantly worked with and managed to see new opportunities in what they have inherited from history's disruptive moments and in that way have overcome the difficulties time has created, Williams says. He goes on, ". . . believers have constantly, if not reinvented the Church, then at least rediscovered and redefined its essence"[19] but adds that this has not always been the way to understand our history. It is the difficulty in arriving at a proper—disturbing but developing—understanding of the relation between our history and the past that is the subject of Williams' book. He presents a picture of difficulties in refraining from using history simply as a toolbox for one's own ends. History either becomes something that can never be reached in any way, and therefore nothing to look back on, or it will turn into the master design on which everything in the future is going to be modelled. Williams sees both approaches in church history and in present times, but does not approve of either. Instead he wants to understand history as something that meets us with its otherness, something strange and disturbing; something that forces us out of our comfort zone and challenges us in a fundamental way. But at the same time he understands history as something possible to work with and to understand in some form. History is not something completely alien and totally incomprehensible. There is a constant tension.

Time after time through Christian history people have faced situations that involve a major break with tradition. The Bible is full of such stories, says Williams; it provides examples of how people who confront disruptive events try to understand and reformulate what was previously thought into new forms. The Jewish people have, for example, been forced to reformulate God's will with them in their understanding of the exodus and the exile. The early Christians had to rethink or reformulate their beliefs, time after

---

19. Williams, *Why Study the Past?* 113.

time. Not least in their thoughts about the coming of the Messiah or their thoughts about their relation to the Jewish community.[20]

> To approach the texts of our history trying to avoid either distorting or patronising is not easy. And we are brought back here to some of the very basic issues with which this investigation began. We are liable to erode the real difference between present and past, ignoring what makes past genuinely strange to us; we are equally liable to treat the past simply as a set of inadequate attempts to think or do what we now know how to think and do. But a theologically intelligent reading of our history requires something more serious. For a grasp of real difference as well as real continuity, we need what de Lubac calls the critic; we need to allow critical scholarship to suspect and turn inside out what is before us, to do its worst; but we cannot lose sight of the fact that, if this history is indeed ours, to examine it is to examine our own identity.[21]

So conversations between historical times are possible, according to Williams, but not in a simple way. Rather it needs work and an awareness that there may be no unequivocal answers. Good historical writing is something that enhances my understanding of my identity; something that links my present identity to a great many different things in history, some of which I understand, some of which I find incomprehensible. But what I do and what I do not understand are both parts of my identity.[22] Bad historical writing, on the other hand, is for Williams: ". . . any kind of narrative that refuses this difficulty and enlargement—either by giving us a version of the past that is just the present in fancy dress or by dismissing the past as a wholly foreign country whose language we shall never learn. . ."[23] Bad historical writing does not improve our identity; instead, by reducing the strangeness of our history and thereby preventing us from comparing ourselves with historical thoughts and actions and so locking us into our own time, it makes it more difficult for us to understand who we are. Bad history does not challenge us.

> Good history is irreducibly a moral affair . . . but in the very least in persuading us to put some distance between ourselves and ourselves, between our imagination and what we habitually take for

---

20. Ibid., 6.
21. Ibid, 101–2.
22. Ibid, 23–24.
23. Ibid, 24.

granted. Its effect may be radical or conservative: it may stir up in us a sense of real anxiety about what is at risk in the comfortable atmosphere of liberal modernity, it may expose the ways in which what seemed absolutely given and unarguable has prevented us from grasping that the way things are is the result of a process, not a natural law. History will not tell us then what to do, but will at least start us on the road to action that is moral in a way it can't be if we have no points of reference beyond what we have come to take for granted.[24]

Williams rejects both the view that history cannot be reached, it is too far away, and the view that history is normative for our lives today. Instead he points to the constant tension between them. I am who I am because of others; I belong to the body of Christ, but so do the people of history. ". . . I should at least be thinking of my identity as a believer in terms of a whole immeasurable exchange of gifts, known and unknown, by which particular Christian lives are built up . . ."[25] In that way we are always in debt to others whom we do not control. Others on whom God's sanctifying grace is also working. And they too have answered God's call and tried to respond to it, just as we do. Therefore it is not enough, according to Williams, to say that the Christians of today know more than Christians in earlier times and therefore they are of no use to us; neither is it enough to say that what history tells is enough for us today.[26] But managing this requires an effort. ". . . God speaks in a manner that insists we continue to grow in order to hear."[27] To believe in a revealed religion means that history and everything it contains are not something the believer can choose to dialogue with or not. In a revealed religion we are ". . . bound to this demanding conversation, this mutual questioning of past and present, in which we discover more fully what we are as a community and who we are as baptised Christians. Out of this, we hope, comes a more mature skill in listening and conversing now."[28]

As said above, the difficulties and problems Williams addresses seem to be present in this material. One indication is that the churches use of their Lutheran heritage, or their interpretation of it, normally seems to be in line with the individual church's general vision and convictions. In

24. Ibid, 24–25.
25. Ibid., 27.
26. Ibid., 27–28.
27. Ibid., 112.
28. Ibid.

other words, theology seems to have difficulties in functioning as a critical correlation in upcoming situations. The material can at least elicit an apprehension that this could happen in the churches. There are signs in the material that the doctrine of the two kingdoms, for example, could be used both as a way to criticise the government, as the rather liberal ILCO does in Costa Rica, and as a way to stay out of political discussions, like the more conservative FLM in Madagascar. Or that the view on vocation can differ, from backing up a rather conservative way of living in one church and at the same time, in another church, be accustomed to seeing men and women as free and responsible, religiously, politically and socially. Both examples suggest that the interpretation of the Lutheran heritage in each church is very much in line with that church's general outlook. The point is that the material gives no clear indications that any of the churches have had more critical deliberations on how to let the Lutheran heritage guide what they are doing. They are mainly looking to their Lutheran heritage for confirmation, not for a critical challenge. A serious critical dialogue with the Lutheran heritage, a dialogue that opens for real changes, has been hard to find. That goes for all five churches, be they large or small, conservative or liberal, young or old, Charismatic or mainline. The Lutheran heritage is there to be seen, albeit vaguely articulated, but it seems to function preferably as something that legitimizes, rather than criticizing, the prevalent opinion. There is, of course, nothing unique or strange about this; it happens all the time in every church. At the same time it is both problematic and dangerous. Problematic because it puts theology in the position of being just a tool for what one wants to hear, not a serious critical dialogue with the word of God. Dangerous because it opens up for the possibility of legitimizing whatever people want the church to stand for. To improve this critical dialogue with the historical tradition and afford help in a difficult task, the dialogue could be extended to include perspectives from other Lutheran churches.

A Need for a Critical Dialogue with Other Lutheran Churches

The critical dialogue with tradition is most important for a prosperous combination of a *semper reformanda* and a confessional understanding of the tradition, but this study has shown that a constructive, critical dialogue with history, context, and tradition is difficult to achieve. The dialogue with tradition and context tends to be undertaken within a church and it would probably be beneficial if churches did not try to tackle this task on their own. To be able to handle their own heritage in constructive and critical ways they need to be in dialogue with other churches. Opinions about how to act and handle can also deepen and become more complex through a critical dialogue with other contemporary attempts to take the shared tradition seriously.

Perhaps, as this study has shown, this insight—that churches need each other, not just to help each other, but also to come to a better understanding of themselves and their situation—is one of the most important reasons for having an interest, not just in differences between traditions and confessions, but also in differences—and an awareness of problems—in one's own tradition.

CHALLENGES FOR THE FUTURE

Five hundred years have passed since the Reformation and Lutheranism is now a global phenomenon. The Lutheran tradition has never been uniform—neither then nor today—but it does provide important tools for dealing with or unlocking what is restricting people, systems and societies. But in order to perform that function in a reflective and critical way, the tradition must be known—and constantly elaborated.

Some of what this study has revealed could best be described as challenges to Lutheran churches to succeed in this.

The Importance of Taking the Situation Seriously

The study has revealed that all five churches are involved in handling problems that often turn out to be dilemmas. There are many things that affect them in handling those dilemmas, some internal, others external. But they clearly endeavor to act so that the situations are addressed as well as possible. They are struggling to be responsible and relevant in their respective situations. This means that they see the importance of not just applying theology but of doing theology in the situation, thereby creating a contextual theology.

Most people are aware that every church operates in a contextual situation and brings with it a certain history, structure and ties to society. Still, it is all too easy to see other churches in the light of one's own church, making it easy to criticize what one sees in other churches. What this study shows is that such criticism easily misses the target. No church in the study is working ad hoc; they all have good reasons for acting as they do. Of course that does not mean one should refrain from criticism. To be fruitful, however, a dialogue is needed about what is seen as problematic in a church, knowing that what someone sees as problematic is probably—or at least could be—that church's way of handling dilemmas in the best way, due to context and history. Criticizing one another, when appropriate, is important but it is just as important that the critic has an open mind and understands that another church's answer to a given question may be well thought-out even if the answer differs from what the critic's would have been.

Once again, this does not mean that there is no right or wrong or that criticism is never appropriate. Instead, it argues for the importance of having an open attitude when others appear to be going in a direction that from the outside seems to be wrong, and of understanding that, from their point of view, their reasons for doing what they are doing may well be sound.

The Importance of Using Tradition as a Critical Partner

The study shows that the churches are trying to be responsible and relevant and to be that in an authentic way. But what is understood as Lutheran tends to be seen, in a non-problematized way, as in line with their own arguments. Lutheranism then becomes something that provides evidence for one's opinion, more seldom something that problematizes and questions it.

It is therefore a challenge to maintain a constant, critical dialogue with tradition. Both a *semper reformanda* and a confessional understanding of the tradition must be there to inform one another. But to achieve this and remain in a constant critical dialogue between them, there needs to be an honest conversation. And to facilitate that conversation, it could be helpful to have a conversation with other churches' attempts to handle the shared tradition.

The Importance of a Constant, Ongoing Conversation

All churches have important contributions to share with other churches. The questions one church is struggling with are probably not confined to that Church; they are matters that other churches also face. A constant, open and positive dialogue is therefore highly important in order to learn from each other's experiences. There is no simple way for churches to check what it means to be Lutheran. If that were the case, a simple manual would suffice. The study shows that what it means to be a Lutheran church is a complex, constantly evolving matter. In constructing their future, churches need other churches' opinions, not primarily as criticism but as voices which help each other to grow and mature in their specific contexts. But it is not just the dialogue between churches in the same denomination that is important. An ongoing dialogue is also greatly needed between churches of different denominations, between religions, between our world today and history, between churches and society and not least between individuals in the congregations, between lay people and ordained, between young and old and between those who are conservative and those who are progressive.

Meeting the Challenges

The results of this study calls for further academic research into Lutheran theology. The study also indicates that work and research are needed on what it means to be a Lutheran church in an ecumenical setting. Perhaps most importantly, this study calls for further discussion about new and improved ways of forming reflective practitioners,[29] on both an individual and a congregational level. Individuals, congregations, and churches need to find ways of relating their realities to their traditions, and also of relating to other churches' attempts to handle the relation between their heritage, tradition and context.

The use of four theologians in this study—Bonhoeffer, Sykes, Niebuhr, and Moltmann—and five churches—the IECLB, the ILCO, the ELCI, the FLM, and the HKBP—is intended to help towards such a conversation. This methodological approach indicates that new perspectives can be illuminated and that theological conversations can guide and enrich churches' decisions on a general level.

Ultimately, to be able to do relevant academic research, to be constructive in ecumenical dialogues and to be able to correlate one's own tradition with the context, everything points to the need of good, relevant training at universities, seminars, and parishes. This is probably the most important factor for a prosperous future for Lutheran churches around the globe. If churches want to be responsible and relevant and to be that authentically, theological education must likewise be authentically responsible and relevant. Here every church has a responsibility not only to do its best but also to help other churches in relevant ways with critical and encouraging

---

29. See for example: Schön, *Reflective Practitioner* or Schön, *Educating the Reflective Practitioner.*

advice and discussions so that practical church life in a true sense is in a position to undertake historical and global theological reflection.

Appendix, Questionnaire

The general questions put to the informants are listed below under five headings. The questions were put in an open way, giving the informants an opportunity to elaborate the response as they wished. Depending on the responses, different questions were put to follow up what had been said.

1. Background
   - Can you give me a general view of your church? Do you think there are other and different views?
   - Are there "things"—ideas or theology—in your church which you do not understand or do not approve of?
   - Do you think of your church as "one", or is it divided in some way? If it is divided, what are the reasons, according to you? Is it grounded in theology or does it have other reasons?
   - What roll does the church service play in your church, practically and theologically?
   - What challenges can you see for your church in the future—from society, from other churches or from inside your church?
   - How would you describe the government/leadership of your church?
   - Can you describe the kind of people who are active in your church (sex, age, race, economic class, other)? Why do you think it is them and not others who belong to your church?
   - What roll do you think your church plays in people's ordinary life?
   - Do you think "democracy" is a useful/important term in describing the inner life of a church?

- What are the relations between your church and other Christian denominations?
- What are the relations between your church and other religions?

2. Lutheran Identity
    - What does it mean to you to be a Lutheran church? What are the theological characteristics? What can be "changed" and what cannot?
    - Is it at all important to be a Lutheran church? Why?
    - How would you present the most central parts of Lutheran theology? Do you think that what you just said are also the most important parts of your church's theology?
    - In what way would you say that it is possible to see that your church is a Lutheran church?

3. Pentecostal or Charismatic Influences
    - In what way—if any—have pentecostal, neopentecostal, or charismatic movements influenced your church? What happens with service, dress code, and church life in general? Have there been splits?
    - Do you think pentecostal or charismatic movements are good or bad for the future development of your church? How come?
    - Are there things from the pentecostal or charismatic tradition that your church has absorbed. If so how come?

4. Situation for Women
    - How would you describe the situation for women in your church?
    - Compared with the society in which your church exists, would you say that women and men are more or less equal in the church that in society as a whole?
    - Why is this so? What is it in your church that promotes equality/work against equality?
    - Is the role of women something you have been discussing and paid attention to in your church?

- Is there a theological underpinning/reason for the role of women *vis-à-vis* men in your church? In your society?

5. Present-Day "Burning Issues"
   - How would you describe the present-day "burning issues" for your church?
   - How does that relate to burning issues in society in general?

Sources and Bibliography

UNPRINTED SOURCES

The materials under this heading are to be found at the archive of this book's author, and are listed as "UP" in the footnotes.

Aritonang, Jan. "Some Notes on the Confession of HKBP."
———. "The Influence and Impact of Charismatic Movements on the Lutheran Churches in Indonesia."
Bakke, Arild. "Programrapport fra representant, 2010."
Björnsdóttir, Steinunn Arnþrúður. "How Lutheran? The Evangelical Lutheran Church of Iceland in the Light of Statistics from 1986–2005 and Luther's Marks of the Church."
Bóasdóttir, Sólveig Anna. "Den kyrkliga debatten kring registrerat partnerskap och samkönade äktenskap på Island."
"The Church of Iceland." (Un-named and un-dated document).
"Church Profile. Igreja Evangélica de Confissão Luterana no Brasil, (IECLB)—Brasil 2009."
"Den costaricanska lutherska kyrkan." (Un-named and un-dated document).
Fabien, Lotera. "Women's situation in the Malagasy Lutheran Church."
"Gender Equality Plan, ELCI." (Un-named and un-dated document).
Gierus, Renate. "Joint Research Project Between the Swedish Church and the Lutheran Church in Costa Rica (ILCO)."
"God's Mission. The IECLB Missionary Action Plan 2008–2012—Base text."
Hedqvist. "ILCO (Iglesia Lutherana Cosraricense)—Mission och Vision."
———. "Missionärsrapportering från Costa Rica."
Hugason, Hjalti. "Kyrka-stat relationen i Island—'A Burning Issue'?"
"Kyrkan som vill stå på Livets sida." (Un-named and un-dated document).
Lumbantobing, Darwin. "The Burning Issues in the Lutheran Church in Indonesia."
Mena Oreamuno, Francisco. "ILCO: Spiritual Movement in a Symbiotic Culture."
Pardede, Erlina. "Women in North Sumatra. A long Struggle to Eliminate Injustice and Violence against Women."
"Policy document ELCI, 2003."
Ranarivony, Colette. "The Renewal Movement in the Malagasy Lutheran Church."
Randrianasolo, Joseph. "The Malagasy Lutheran Church: A Church in Mission."
Rasolondraibe, Peri. "Awakening to the Power of God."

Razivelo, Mariette. "Influences of Awakening—'Fifohazana'—and the Globally Growing Neo-Pentecostal Movement in the Churches of Madagascar Today."
Rojas Campbell, Miguel. "A Spirit that Frees from the Closet."
Schmiedt Streck, Valburga, and Marcia Blasi. "Gender Issues and the Evangelical Church of the Lutheran Confession—IECLB."
Schneider, Marcelo. "The Role of Present-day 'Burning Issues' for the Formation and Identity of the IECLB."
"The Malagasy Lutheran Church Vision." (Un-named and un-dated document).
Wachholz, Wilhelm. "Lutheranism in Brazil: Trajectories and Challenges."

INTERVIEWS

The interviews under this heading are to be found at the archive of this book's author.

Costa Rica

Bonilla, Carlos. Pastor. San Jose, June 2009.
Chacón, Xinia. Church official. San Jose, June 2009.
Hedqvist, Katarina. Missionary. San Jose, June 2009.
Hedqvist, Magnus. Missionary. San Jose, June 2009.
Jiménez, Melwin. Bishop of the ILCO. San Jose, June 2009.
Mora, Christina. Member. San Jose, June 2009.
Quesada Mora, Gilberto. Pastor. San Jose, June 2009.

Brazil

Altmann, Walter. President of the IECLB. Porto Alegre, June 2009.
Blasi, Marcia. Pastor/Researcher. São Leopoldo, June 2009.
Schmiedt Streck, Valburga. Researcher. São Leopoldo, June 2009.
Souza, Mauro. Researcher. Porto Alegre, June 2009.
Wemuth, Douglas. Pastor. Porto Alegre, June 2009.

Iceland

Björnsdóttir, Steinunn Arnþrúður. Pastor. Reykjavík, May 2009.
Bóasdóttir, Sólveig Anna. Researcher. Reykjavík, May 2009.
Danielsson, Árni Svanur. Pastor. Reykjavík, May 2009.
Guðmundsdóttir, Arnfríður. Researcher. Reykjavík, May 2009.
Hugason, Hjalti. Researcher. Reykjavík, May 2009.
Kristjánsson, Gunnar. Pastor. In the outskirts of Reykjavík, May 2009.
Þórðarson, Sigurður Árni. Pastor. Reykjavík, May 2009.
Vilhjálmsdóttir, Auður Eir. Pastor. Reykjavík, May 2009.

Madagascar

Bakke, Arild. Missionary. Antananarivo, June 2010.
Endor Modeste, Rakoto. President of the FLM. Antananarivo, June 2010.

Fabien, Lotera. Researcher. Fianarantsoa, June 2010.
Randrianasolo, Joseph. Researcher. Fianarantsoa, June 2010.
Rasolondraibe, Peri. Pastor. Antananarivo, June 2010.
Razivelo, Mariette. Researcher. Fianarantsoa, June 2010.

Indonesia

Aritonang, Jan. Researcher. Medan, November 2010.
Damanik, Janri. LWF employed. Medan, November 2010.
Lumbantobing, Darwin. Researcher. Medan, November 2010.
Nainggolan, Binsar. Church official. Tarutung, November 2010.
Pardede, Erlina. Researcher. Medan, November 2010.

BIBLIOGRAPHY

Althaus, Paul. *The Theology of Martin Luther*. Philadelphia: Fortress, 1966.
Altmann, Walter. *Luther and Liberation: A Latin American Perspective*. Minneapolis: Fortress, 1992.
"Arbeta som präst," http://www.svenskakyrkan.se/default.aspx?id=642913.
Aurelius, Carl Axel. *Luther i Sverige: Svenska lutherbilder under tre sekler*. Skellefteå: Artos, 1994.
Billing, Einar. *Den svenska folkkyrkan*. Stockholm: Sveriges kristliga studentrörelses förlag, 1930.
Blåder, Niclas. *Gemenskap och mångfald: En ekklesiologisk studie med med utgångspunkt i Don S. Brownings metod, där två församlingars tal om identitet och pluralism i den egna församlingen relateras till Dietrich Bonhoeffers teologiska tänkande*. Linköping Studies in Arts and Science 452. Linköping: Linköpings universitet, 2008.
Bonhoeffer, Dietrich. *Life Together*. Dietrich Bonhoeffer Works 5. Edited by Geffrey B. Kelly, 27–118. Minneapolis: Fortress, 2005.
Browning, Don S. *A Fundamental Practical Theology: Descriptive and Strategic Proposals*. Minneapolis: Fortress, 1996.
Chung, Paul, et al. *Liberating Lutheran Theology: Freedom for Justice and Solidarity in a Global Context*. Minneapolis: Fortress, 2011.
The Church of Sweden Act. SFS 1998:1591. http://www.sweden.gov.se/sb/d/3926/a/27832.
Claesson, Urban. "Att lösa klimatproblem med Luther eller Calvin: Reflektioner om det typiskt svenska som uttryck för en sekulariserad teologi." In *Luther som utmaning: Om frihet och ansvar*, edited by Elisabeth Gerle, 183–99. Stockholm: Verbum, 2008.
Deifelt, Wanda. "The Relevance of the Doctrine of Justification." In *Justification in the World's Context*, edited by Wolfgang Greive, 33–42. LWF Documentation 45. Geneva: Lutheran World Federation, 2000.
Eckerdal, Jan. *Folkkyrkans kropp: Einar Billings ecklesiologi i postsekulär belysning*. Skellefteå: Artos, 2012.
———. "Om att lära sig vara i minoritet—men ändå vara glad: Missionsformad kyrka i en efterkristen tid." In *I rörelse: Fyra artiklar om kyrkans mission skrivna för präst och diakonmötet 2013 i Strängnäs stift*, edited by Anna S. Wikell, 10–38. Skellefteå: Artos, 2013.

Effendi, Djohan. "Reconciliation in the Indonesian Context." In *Dialogue and Beyond: Christians and Muslims Together on the Way*, edited by Sigvard von Sicard & Ingo Wulfhorst, 113–16. LWF Studies 1. Geneva: Lutheran World Federation, 2003.

Ekelund, Jan-Anders, and Håkan Sunnliden. "Bekännelseskrifterna och ekumeniska överenskommelser." Motion 2010:40. *Svenska kyrkan*. July 10, 2010. http://svenskakyrkan.se/default.aspx?id=674602.

Ekstrand, Thomas. "The Construction of Lutheran Identity in Church of Sweden." In *Exploring a Heritage: Evangelical Lutheran Churches in the North*, edited by Anne-Louise Eriksson, et al., 249–64. Eugene, OR: Pickwick, 2012.

Eriksson, Anne-Louise, et al., editors. *Exploring a Heritage: Evangelical Lutheran Churches in the North*. Eugene, OR: Pickwick, 2012.

Eriksson, Anne-Louise, et al. *Demokratin är en successiv uppenbarelse. För utredningen Demokrati och delaktighet i Svenska kyrkan*. Uppsala: Svenska kyrkan, 2005.

Gregersen, Niels Henrik. "Introduction: Ten Theses on the Future of Lutheran Theology." In *The Gift of Grace: The Future of Lutheran Theology*, edited by Niels Henrik Gregersen, et al., 1–14. Minneapolis: Fortress, 2005.

Green, Clifford J. *Bonhoeffer: A Theology of Sociality*. Grand Rapids: Eerdmans, 1999.

Greive, Wolfgang editor. *Between Vision and Reality: Lutheran Churches in Transition*. LWF Documentation 47. Geneva: Lutheran World Federation, 2001.

Gritsch, Eric W. *A History of Lutheranism*. Minneapolis: Fortress, 2010.

Groome, Thomas. *The Way of Shared Praxis: An Approach to Religious Education*. Religionspedagogiska institutets skriftserie 1. Lomma: Religionspedagogiska institutet, 1999.

Gubrium, Jaber F. and James A. Holstein. *The New Language of Qualitative Method*. Oxford: Oxford University Press, 1997.

Gustafsson, Berndt. *Svensk kyrkohistoria*. Helsingborg: Bokförlaget Plus Ultra, 1983.

Holte, Ragnar. *Luther och Lutherbilden. En kritisk granskning*. Stockholm: Proprius, 1984.

Hägglund, Bengt. *Teologins historia: En dogmhistorisk översikt*. Stockholm: Liber förlag, 1984.

Höppner, Reinhard. "Justification and Society." In *Justification in the World's Context*, edited by Wolfgang Greive, 27–32. LWF Documentation 45. Geneva: Lutheran World Federation, 2000.

Ingebrand, Sven. "Olavus Petri—Reformatorn." In *Olaus Petri: Den mångsidige svenske reformatorn*, edited by Carl F. Hallencreutz and Sven-Ola Lindeberg, 13–30. Skrifter utgivna av Svenska Kyrkohistoriska Föreningen 49. Uppsala: Svenska Kyrkohistoriska Föreningen, 1994.

Inglehart, Ronald and Chris Welzel. "The WVS Cultural Map of the World." *World Values Survey*. http://www.worldvaluesurvey.org/wvs.jsp.

Isaak, Paul John. "The Church's Prophetic Witness: Social, Economic, and Political Engagement." In *Theological Practices That Matter*, edited by Karen L. Bloomquist, 143–52. Theology in the Life of the Church 5. Geneva: Lutheran World Federation, 2009.

Jacobsen, Douglas. *The World's Christians: Who they are, Where they are, and How they got there*. Chichester: Wiley-Blackwell, 2011.

Jorgenson, Allen G. "Contours of the Common Priesthood." In *The Global Luther: A Theologian for Modern Times*, edited by Christine Helmer, 249–65. Minneapolis: Fortress, 2009.

Kvale, Steinar. *Den kvalitativa forskningsintervjun*. Lund: Studentlitteratur, 1997.

Kyrkoordningen. Svenska kyrkan. January 1, 2015. http://www.svenskakyrkan.se/kyrkoord ningen.
Lagerquist, L. DeAne, and Caryn D. Riswold. "Historical and Theological Legacies of Feminism and Lutheranism." In *Transformative Lutheran Theologies: Feminist, Womanist, and Mujerista Perspectives,* edited by Mary J. Streufert, 15–30. Minneapolis: Fortress, 2010.
Lindberg, Carter. "Luther's Struggle with Social-Ethical Issues." In *The Cambridge Companion to Martin Luther,* edited by Donald K. McKim, 165–78. Cambridge: Cambridge University Press, 2003.
Lohse, Bernard. *Martin Luther's Theology: Its Historical and Systematic Development.* Minneapolis: Fortress, 2011.
Long, D. Stephen. *Theology and Culture: A Guide to the Discussion.* Eugene, OR: Cascade, 2008.
Martinson, Mattias. *Katedralen mitt i staden: Om ateism och teologi.* Lund: Arcus, 2010.
Moltmann, Jürgen. *The Church in the Power of the Spirit: A Contribution to Messianic Ecclesiology.* Minneapolis: Fortress, 1993.
———. *The Crucified God: The Cross of Christ as the Foundation and Criticism of Christian Theology.* London: SCM, 1974.
———. *Theology of Hope: On the Ground and the Implications of a Christian Eschatology.* London: SCM, 1967.
Niebuhr, H. Richard. *Christ & Culture.* San Francisco: HarperSanFrancisco, 2001.
Nordlander, Leif. "Luther i fem år." Motion 2011:63. *Svenska kyrkan.* July 20, 2010. https://www.svenskakyrkan.se/default.aspx?id=803942.
Nürnberger, Klaus. *Martin Luther's Message for Us Today: A Perspective from the South.* Pietermaritzburg: Cluster, 2005.
"Protestant Christian Batak Church," http://www.oikoumene.org/en/member-churches/protestant-christian-batak-church.
Raunio, Antti. "Luther's Social Theology in the Contemporary World: Searching for the Neighbor's Good." In *The Global Luther. A Theologian for Modern Times,* edited by Christine Helmer, 210–227. Minneapolis: Fortress, 2009.
Roth, Hans Ingvar. *Identitet och pluralism: En forskningsöversikt med särskild hänsyn till religionsvetenskapliga aspekter.* Linköping Studies in Identity and Pluralism 1. Linköping: Linköping University Electronic Press, 2003.
Ryman, Björn, et al. *Nordic Folk Churches: A Contemporary Church History.* Grand Rapids: Eerdmans, 2005.
Schön, Donald A. *Educating the Reflective Practitioner: Toward a New Design for Teaching and Learning in the Professions.* San Francisco: Jossey-Bass, 1987.
———. *The Reflective Practitioner: How Professionals Think in Action.* Basic Books, 1983.
Stolt, Birgit. *Martin Luther. Människohjärtat och bibeln.* Stockholm: Verbum, 1994.
"Svenska kyrkan i siffror," https://svenskakyrkan.se/default.aspx?id=645562.
Sykes, Stephen. *Power and Christian Theology.* London: Continuum, 2006.
"Tillsammans gör vi kyrkovalet," https://www.svenskakyrkan.se/default.aspx?id=581917
van der Ven, Johannes A. *Ecclesiology in Context.* Grand Rapids: Eerdmans, 1996.
Westhelle, Vítor. "Transfiguring Lutheranism: Being Lutheran in New Contexts." In *Identity, Survival Witness: Reconfiguring Theological Agendas,* edited by Karen L. Bloomquist, 11–23. Theology in the Life of the Church 3. Geneva: Lutheran World Federation, 2008.

Williams, Rowan. *Why Study the Past? The Quest for the Historic Church*. Grand Rapids: Eerdmans, 2005.
Wingren, Gustaf. *Luthers lära om kallelsen*. Skellefteå: Artos, 1993.
Wriedt, Markus. "Luther's Theology." In *The Cambridge Companion to Martin Luther*, edited by Donald K. McKim, 86–119. Cambridge: Cambridge University Press, 2003.

www.ingramcontent.com/pod-product-compliance
Lightning Source LLC
Chambersburg PA
CBHW062046220426
43662CB00010B/1673